A LONG WAY FROM SWANSEA

A Memoir

Sir Albert Thomas Lamb
KBE CMG DFC

with a foreword by
the Rt Hon Lord Callaghan of Cardiff KG

Starborn Books

A LONG WAY FROM SWANSEA
Sir Albert Thomas Lamb

First published in 2003
by Starborn Books
Glanrhydwilym, Llandissilio,
Clunderwen SA66 7QH
Pembs., Wales, U.K.

E-mail: sales@starbornbooks.co.uk
Website: www.starbornbooks.co.uk

© Sir Albert Thomas Lamb 2003

Patrick Barrington's poem 'I had a duck-billed platypus' is
reproduced with permission of Punch Ltd.

All rights reserved
Starborn Books 2003

No part of this book may be reproduced, stored in a retrieval system, or transmitted in any form or by any means, electronic, mechanical, photocopying, recording or otherwise without permission in writing from the publisher.

ISBN 1 899530 13 4

CONTENTS

Foreword		7
Preface		11
Chapter 1:	Beginnings	15
Chapter 2:	Royal Air Force	24
Chapter 3:	Foreign Office, Rome and Genoa	47
Chapter 4:	Bucharest	55
Chapter 5:	Foreign Office	61
Chapter 6:	Middle East Centre for Arabic Studies	65
Chapter 7:	Promotion, Bahrain and Trade Promotion	71
Chapter 8:	Foreign Office: The Oil Desk	85
Chapter 9:	Kuwait	93
Chapter 10:	Political Agent in Abu Dhabi	98
Chapter 11:	Diplomatic Service Inspectorate	128
Chapter 12:	Ambassador to Kuwait	136
Chapter 13:	Ambassador to Norway	148
Chapter 14:	Envoi for an Envoy	172

FOREWORD

Archie Lamb's career and his account of life as an Ambassador is a far cry from descriptions of the sophisticated grandeur of our embassies in Paris and Washington. His early story was typical of much of his generation. Born to a working class family, his father dogged by unemployment, ill health and a shortage of money, his family's main concern was to ensure that the children should find a permanent job with a secure pension. According to his headmaster, Archie's ability at school would have ensured a place at Oxford University, but that was no guarantee of security or a pension, whereas the Civil Service promised both.

It is often said nowadays that a so-called "glass ceiling" prevents women from breaking through to the top posts in the professions and businesses, and it is true. Sixty years ago in the Civil Service this was true of men as well as women. The competitive examination system of the day divided recruits to the Civil Service into three distinctive classes: Administrative Class (from the universities), Executive Class (from the grammar schools), and Clerical Class (from the secondary schools). The glass ceiling prevented transfers from a lower to a higher class, and with few exceptions, once a recruit was allocated to the Clerical Class, rarely did he or she escape from it.

Archie Lamb was an exception. Starting in the Clerical Class at the Foreign Office in 1938, in due course he broke through the glass ceiling, becoming a Flight Lieutenant in the Royal Air Force during World War II, when he won the Distinguished Flying Cross, the DFC, followed by senior posts in various Middle East Missions, including Bahrain and Abu Dhabi, and became Ambassador to Kuwait, ending his career as Ambassador to Norway. Michael Palliser, Head of the Diplomatic Service, rightly wrote on the occasion of Archie Lamb's retirement, "Your rise from Clerical Officer to Ambassador has been an inspiration."

It needed World War II to transform the situation, which improved partly as a result of Ernest Bevin's influence, and with the agreement of Anthony Eden. The three main Classes in the Foreign Office were unified and integrated, in the course of which a spring of enterprise and initiative was released in the lower ranks.

After serving in the war, Archie Lamb took full advantage at the Foreign Office of the changes that had been wrought. He was good at languages and, discovering that there was a shortage of Arabic specliaists, enrolled in the School of Oriental and African Studies at London University. In due course his initiative led the Foreign Office to post him to the Middle East, where he spent much of his career, and made full use of his time. His shrewd comments depict a rapidly changing era, during which, as late as the 1960s, a reactionary ruler in the Middle East saw no need for hospitals or schools, and used a suitcase of bank notes to pay the Government's debts. This was at a time when the international oil companies were growing into giants of production and export throughout the whole of the Middle East.

Archie Lamb's book gives us a lively account of events both great and small. For example his wife found, when he was posted to the Gulf, that the accommodation was so spartan that she was forced to retire to her bedroom when notables came to the Residence, as there was only one sitting room.

Archie Lamb is very critical of the oil companies. He speaks of their "political obtuseness" in the 1960s when they disregarded the declared interests of the Arab oil states. He says the American oil companies were as obtuse as the British, French and Dutch, but he adds that the Unites States Government had a much clearer view: "take as much [of the oil] as possible under American control". It was the transformation of America from an exporter of oil to becoming a major importer that resulted in the efforts of the Middle East States to nationalise oil, and led to the formation of OPEC by the Iranian and other Middle Eastern Governments, to much of the political upheaval of the Middle East, and to the great changes that even now are still unfolding.

Much that he says is of importance in understanding the past developments of the Middle East. Archie Lamb's description and personal knowledge give a special authority to his account, which I am sure will be widely read and appreciated.

James Callaghan
April 2003

Dedication

On 29 November 1939, at a Civil Service Ball in London, I met Christina Betty Wilkinson. We married on 8 April 1944 and have lived happily ever after. Her love and support, during the years chronicled in this memoir, have provided the inspiration and support without which I doubt that such success as I enjoyed would have come my way. This is as much Christina's story as mine; it is, in truth, about both of us and can only be dedicated to her.

PREFACE

Whenever, during over forty years service with the Royal Air Force and the Foreign Office, I returned home to Swansea where I was born and educated and where my parents lived, I would be greeted by family, friends and neighbours with "Hello, boy! Home again! When you going back? Long way from Swansea now, aren't you?"

This memoir is an attempt to answer those friendly questions more fully than I did at the time.

A LONG WAY FROM SWANSEA

1

Beginnings

I was born in Swansea on 23 October 1921, the first child and elder son of Reginald Selwyn and Violet Lamb (née Haynes), who later added a second son (on my birthday three years later) and a daughter (twelve years later) to their family. My parents were "of humble origin", a phrase I came to know much later when I was working in the Personnel Department of the Foreign Office. My mother had first seen my father as he marched off to the Great War as a Private in the Welch Regiment. "Who is that little boy?" (he stood 5'2") she asked her mother; "Mrs Lamb's boy", came the reply. "Oh, I could not marry anyone called Lamb," said my mother. But she did; and remained happily married to him for fifty years until his death. They married in 1920 on almost nothing and at a time when my father was in and out of hospitals receiving treatment for the wounds and gassing he had suffered during the War. Having joined up under age he had had little formal education, and when I was born he was working as a storekeeper for a firm of general merchants. Later he was a night-watchman, an electrician and, for most of his working life, a commercial traveller selling wireless sets and, later, television sets all over Wales for the Southend-on-Sea-based company of E K Cole, who produced the well-known EKCO sets. One of my earliest memories is listening to the wireless, not from an EKCO or any other commercially-made set, but from one made by my father using a galvanised iron bucket as a loudspeaker.

At the time we were still living with my maternal grandparents, in whose house I had been born. To this day I do not understand the economics of that family, who occupied a beautiful three-storey (with basement) terrace house on the wages of a dock labourer. My grandfather, Albert James Haynes, was the grandson of farm labourers who had emigrated from Mudford in Somerset to Newport in South Wales in the middle of the 19th

Century when the industrial revolution was drawing workers north across the Bristol Channel. His father was a marine engineer, but my grandfather apparently had little or no education. He married my grandmother, Elizabeth Hannah Evans, the daughter of a collier from the Rhondda Valley, when he was 21 and she 19. She always impressed me as being better informed than my grandfather, perhaps the result of regular Welsh chapel-going not practised by her English-born husband. She was the last native Welsh-speaker in our family.

I never knew my Grandfather Lamb, a ship steward, since he was drowned in an accident on the River Thames at Becton (Woolwich) in 1901 at the age of 41 when my father was only 18 months old. Grandmother Lamb (née Thomas) was left with six children and no income. She took a stall in Swansea Market selling poultry and eggs and made enough money, augmented by the earnings of her elder children, to keep her home and her family together proudly and without complaint. As a small child my Saturday treat was to visit Grannie Lamb at her stall in the Market, and on Sunday we all repaired to her house for tea (invariably tinned salmon and jelly, I remember) where, as a true matriarch, she was attended by her six children, their spouses and offspring. She sat in a corner of her parlour, with her feet on a footstool, dressed all in black with a white lace cap on her head. We all went into the parlour in turn by families to greet her and to answer her enquiries about our health, wealth and education.

My mother, the wife of her youngest child, was a favourite of Grannie Lamb and was always invited back into the parlour to sit beside her mother-in-law after the family obeisances were complete. My mother's formal education ended, because of illness, when she was eleven years old. Neither lack of education nor ill-health in childhood reduced her ability to bear and bring up three children, cope with the consequences of a prolonged period of ill-health suffered by my father in his forties and never fail to make the apt comment on any matter of passing family or public interest. She felt keenly the pain of my father's death and retired into her own house for two years in mourning for her partner of 50 years, declining all invitations from my brother and myself to come away for a holiday. Then one day, when my brother was home on leave from Tokyo, where he was stationed as ICI's Manager of its Far East interests, she responded positively to his suggestion that she spend Christmas with him in Japan. From that moment, the pain of Father's death having at last become bearable, she became a great traveller, including visits to Kuwait and Oslo in her itinerary before she died at the age of 83.

My parents eventually became eligible for a Council house on the Mayhill Estate in Swansea. If this was not sufficiently exciting my father also acquired a motorcycle and sidecar (or, more accurately, a side-box) which carried us on the first of our many visits to the sweeping bays of the Gower Peninsula, the first officially-proclaimed area of outstanding natural beauty, and elsewhere in Wales. A motorcar soon succeeded the motorcycle when my father obtained employment with E K Cole, who provided a company car. London now featured in our travels since every year we accompanied my father to the Radio Show at Earls Court where, with his fellow salesmen, he was on duty on the EKCO stand. Here I first saw the miracle of television and learned by heart the theme song, sung by Carl Bernard, of the Radio Show of the Thirties:

> "O! O! You Radio
> You are the only friend I know
> When I find you inside my room
> You dispel all the gloom.
> You bring me music, laughter
> Songs I never knew
> O! Radio I'm radiating thanks to you!"

The advent of wireless broadcasting certainly dispelled any gloom there might have been in the Lamb family since it brought a salaried, pensionable employment to my father and, after rented accommodation in Cardiff and Swansea, enabled my parents in 1933 to put down a deposit of £50 and accept a 95% mortgage for a £650 semi-detached, three-bedroom house at Tycoch, three miles to the west of Swansea. That house remained the Lamb home for 47 years until my Mother's death.

In the same year, 1933, I scraped through the 11-plus to win a place in Swansea Grammar School. I was on the borderline after the written examination and was summoned for interview at the School. All I can remember of that interview is that someone asked me what happens to the electricity after it had passed from the overhead wires into one of Swansea's tramcars. I replied that it was used up and so, I suppose, persuaded the interview board to give me a place in the School.

I thoroughly enjoyed the Grammar School, where I had a pleasing scholastic record of only twice falling below the top position in my form. I found that I had been well-prepared in the three R's at Terrace Road Primary School, which I attended between the ages of five and eleven; and the Grammar School introduced me to the further delights of English and to the hitherto unknown excitement of foreign languages. Two of the language teachers were named D J Thomas: "junior", to whom I owe a lot for his inspiring guidance, taught French, German and Spanish and later left teaching to become a producer on BBC Radio; whilst "senior" was the senior English Master and the father of the poet Dylan Thomas, who had also attended Swansea Grammar School. My only memory of D J Thomas Senior is of his sweeping into a classroom with gown afloat calling "Some boy open a window! The room smells like a brothel!" suggesting that DJ knew something we pupils did not.

When, in 1985, I began gathering material for this book, I wrote to the Director of Education of the City of Swansea enquiring if a history of Swansea Grammar School existed and whether I might be permitted to examine the school records for the years 1933 to 1938 during which I was a pupil at the School. I did not receive a reply, not even an acknowledgement; but over one month later I received from the Hon Secretary of the Old Boys Association a helpful letter enclosing a history of the School, now called The Bishop Gore Comprehensive School, which he had written to mark the 300th Anniversary in 1983 of the foundation of the School by Bishop Gore with the motto of "Virtue and Good Literature". (In later years I recognised this motto as a good guide for diplomats). The Hon Secretary explained in his letter that my letter to the Education Authority had been passed to him one calendar month after I wrote it, and that the Authority had no records covering my time at the Grammar School. Presumably the School records were destroyed during a heavy bombing raid on Swansea during the Second World War when the School building suffered irreparable damage. If this presumption is correct, the Education Authority might have exerted itself and told me so. But, clearly, the Education Authority had abandoned, if it had ever practised, the common courtesy of the public service of sending a prompt acknowledgement of receipt of a letter pending a substantive reply. This incident confirmed that I had indeed travelled "a long way from Swansea", in whose educational and correspondence records I was clearly a "non-person".

My schooling ended a year after I had taken School Certificate Credits (what have become known as "O" Levels) in six subjects: English, French, German, Spanish, History and Mathematics. Although E K Cole had been understanding and reasonably generous to my father during a prolonged bout of ill health, money had been short in the Lamb Family. My father therefore decided that I should have to seek paid employment, since he could not see his way to further supporting me as a student at the Grammar School and certainly not at Oxford, where it was the wish of my Headmaster, J Grey Morgan, that I should proceed to study foreign languages at Jesus College, and with a State Scholarship. He failed to persuade my father to reconsider his decision, and when I was sixteen I was entered for the Civil Service Examination for the Clerical Class. The aim of nearly every family in South Wales in the 1930s was to obtain permanent pensionable employment for their children, an aim that could certainly be achieved in the Civil Service. I passed high enough in the examination to be asked which Government Department I would wish to serve in. Knowing, along with my family, nothing of Government Departments, I wrote on the appropriate form that I would like to serve where I could pursue my interest in foreign languages, and so I was appointed a Clerical Officer in the Foreign Office, where I started work on 19 December 1938 at the age of 17 years and 2 months.

There were at that time two Clerical Classes in the Civil Service, General and Departmental, the first presumably indicating that one might serve in any Department and the second that one would serve in one Department only. The General Class, to which I was appointed, paid more, £85 a year against £75 a year for the Departmental. To ease my way into London my father found enough money to subsidise me to lodgings, "digs" in Bedford Square, Bloomsbury, where for 35 shillings a week I shared a room with another young man and was fed breakfast and dinner. Since 35 shillings a week was 2s6d more than my income I soon had to move to cheaper lodgings in Herne Hill, where I obtained the same benefits for 25 shillings a week, the remaining 7s6d covering my rail fares and my lunches, which impecunious young clerks like myself could enjoy at Civil Service canteens around Whitehall for as low as 6d. But I readily admit that at times we went hungry.

My work in the Foreign Office was that of a filing clerk in the Registry, taking files out of boxes, attaching new papers, and later returning them to their boxes after they had been seen by (to me) invisible diplomats and consular officers in Foreign Office Departments, checked in the Registry for the completeness of the action, Name Indexed and Subject Indexed. The Foreign Office being a historical Department of State, great care was taken at that time with the keeping of the papers, the Librarian of the Foreign Office enjoying the additional title of Keeper of the Papers. Under him, and responsible for the correct handling of current files, was the Registrar - a Mr French, when I reported in December 1938 - an important official with his own room just inside the front door of the Office. The Registry was divided into Divisions, each Division working to and for a Department. I worked in the Treaty Division and the Consular Division, not so busy or crisis-ridden at that time as the Central Division, which served the Central Department whose responsibility was Britain's relations with Germany and Austria. The Registries and their clerks, a Higher Clerical Officer in charge of each Division, and a Section Clerk with a £30 per annum French allowance in charge of papers required by one or more desk officers in the Department, existed to serve their departments. There was no feeling that Diplomats, Consular Officers and Clerical Officers were all of the same service: the filing clerks in the Registry had a distinct and separate responsibility in which the departmental officers had no part: the proper keeping of the papers and their production with precedents and references attached when required. The Subject Index, known as the Main Index, of the Office was staffed by clerks, historians manqués, who recorded the substance of the correspondence in a way which would enable particular subjects, precedents or references to be traced in later years by and in, for example, the Public Records Office. The clerks in the Divisions carried out the indexing of names, which occurred in correspondence or interdepartmental minuting. This system was effective and ensured that the Office carried out its statutory duty as an historical Department of State. But whether it was efficient was debatable since it could only operate if it employed educated and intelligent clerks, all of whom, I would say, would have had no difficulty in the easier financial arrangements of later years in securing a place at and graduating with honours from University.

Thirty years later, when I became Chief Inspector of the Diplomatic Service, I discovered that the elaborate system of paper-keeping which I have described, had finally been abandoned and a system, which I can only describe as "paper-gathering", had been imposed on the Office by the Treasury without any protest by the top of the Office, and over the objections of the then Registrar who knew the business of the archivist somewhat better than his superiors, at that time products of the post-war Reconstructions examinations, who had been given the view from the bridge immediately upon entry and had no knowledge or experience of the "engine-room". The Main and Name Indexes had been abolished and it had become impossible to trace references and precedents through the system. Since the status of the Registry had been consistently down-graded, not to say denigrated, since the War and "diplomats" allowed to interfere with something that they did not understand, the professional pride of the archivist had been replaced by the desire of all the filing clerks to get out of Registry work. Hence no continuity and no interest in the work, which would, as it did before the War, make the Registry Clerks as expert on the substance of their subjects as were their departmental superiors.

I hope that nothing I have said about Registry work has suggested that before the War it was a dead-end job: on the contrary. A registry clerk could look forward to an overseas appointment as the Archivist of one of Her Majesty's Diplomatic Missions, and later as the Superintending Archivist of one of the larger and more important Missions, in which capacity he continued to practice the art of paper-keeping while at the same time being introduced to the science (as it is now called) of management. The management/administration of a Mission was the responsibility of the Head of Chancery. Until 1948 the Archivist would have assisted him, but in that year another decision by the Foreign Office downgraded the status of the Archivist and the scope of his task. After the War a retired Colonel was brought into the Office to run a new Department called Conference and Supply. The pre-War diplomats who were then running the Office valued his advice on management and administration, including its application to HM Missions overseas, in which he had never served. Having been raised in the military tradition the good Colonel imagined that, as in the Army, there had to be a distinct rank and function for every task. And so one winter afternoon in 1948 in the room of the Permanent Under Secretary a new bureaucrat, additional to the establishment of a Mission, the Administration Officer, was created and inserted into the hierarchy of a Mission between the Head of Chancery and the Archivist. Parkinson's Law applied with an explosion in the volumes of administrative practice (which became known as Diplomatic Service Procedure) considered necessary to regulate the management of the Foreign Office and Diplomatic Service, or Foreign Service as it was called for a time after World War 2.

All this was in the future when I was working in the Foreign Office, from 1938 to 1941. I volunteered and was accepted for Royal Air Force aircrew duties upon the outbreak of War in September 1939, but was not called up until early 1941.

Meanwhile, I continued my education by reading widely, but particularly biography, history and politics, and joined the Foreign Office Unit of the Local Defence Volunteers (LDV), later renamed the Home Guard on the orders of Prime Minister Winston Churchill to War Minister Anthony Eden. In preparation for repelling the Nazi invader from the Foreign Office premises we spent pleasant Saturdays at the Foreign Office sports ground at Swakeleys near Uxbridge marching up and down in ill-fitting denim khaki uniforms under the command of a pipe-smoking member of the Communications Department who had served in the First World War, and some of our evenings in the basement of the Office being instructed in unarmed self-defence by two constables of the Metropolitan Police who appeared to be convinced that the Wehrmacht would come at us with knives. More realistically the Foreign Office Home Guard were responsible for fire-watching and I saw a lot of the Blitz on London in 1940 and early 1941 from the roof of the Foreign Office, including the evening when the Luftwaffe scored a direct hit on the House of Commons in the Palace of Westminster - a spectacular sight. The Foreign Office building escaped any direct damage during the bombing raids.

I met, on 29 November 1939, at a Civil Service Dance at Bush House in the Strand, Miss Christina Betty Wilkinson, also aged 18, a tax clerk in the Inland Revenue. A mutual friend escorted Miss Wilkinson to the Dance; I escorted her home. We were married on 8 April 1944. The love and support that Christina has given me is the mainspring of this story.

2

Royal Air Force

I received my commission in 1942 at the end of my pilot training in Rhodesia under the Empire Flying Training Scheme at the same time as I was awarded my Royal Air Force pilot's wings by the Rhodesian Group Captain commanding the Royal Rhodesian Air Force Station at Thornhill, near a "one-horse" town called Gwelo, about which the airmen had composed a ribald and unprintable song.

So I moved up from being 1386720 Acting Sergeant Unpaid (ASU), the rank given to officer cadets in Rhodesia, to being 128643 Pilot Officer. I never received any document supporting or certifying my entitlement to commissioned rank, but I did receive a uniform allowance of £15 or £20 and unseen hands in some RAF pay office adjusted my pay.

Having somewhat unwillingly taken leave of Christina in London, I had come to Rhodesia and Thornhill by way of London's Regents Park Zoo, the Hotel Majestic in Torquay, a troopship from Glasgow to Durban, railway from Durban to Bulawayo, three months in a pigpen on the agricultural showground of that Rhodesian town and two months of ab initio flying on Tiger Moths at the Elementary Flying Training School at Guinea Fowl.

I was working in the Foreign Office (of which more later) in London and living in digs at Herne Hill near Dulwich when the Second World War broke out on 3 September 1939. With my cousin Douglas Lamb and our good friend John Meredith Roberts (we had been at Swansea Grammar School together) I volunteered for pilot training the next day but was not called up until 1941, presumably because Britain was woefully short of flying training facilities and had to await the capacity provided by the

Empire Flying Training Scheme to train the thousands of pilots and other aircrew it required to prosecute the War. Unglamorously our RAF career started at London Zoo where we were ordered to report for enlistment, RAF number, uniform, inoculations (many!) and posting orders. We slept on the floor in an unoccupied and unfurnished apartment block near the zoo and ate in the Zoo Restaurant.

It was generally accepted among the recruits that the animals in the zoo could not have been given such deplorable food as we suffered during our time at Regents Park. When we took our turn at kitchen duty some of us were made physically sick by the smell, one could say stench, of the food preparation. We were also kept standing around for hours; by singing that immortal refrain of the Forces "Why are we waiting? O! Why are we waiting?" to the tune of "O! Come all ye faithful", we accomplished all three of relieving our feelings, registering a protest and annoying the NCOs in charge of us. Relief soon came with my transfer, along with 49 other AC2s whose surname began with the letters K, L or M, to C Flight of No. 1 Squadron of No. 5 Initial Training Wing at Torquay in Devon for six weeks of "square-bashing" and introductory lectures on the Royal Air Force, aircraft recognition and navigation. I had always found mathematics difficult at school; but navigation exercises seemed to me comprehensible and enjoyable: from that time at Torquay I have been numerate. We were billeted in the Hotel Majestic, with beds to sleep on and good food to eat. These six weeks made us all proud of our bearing, uniform (we now wore in our caps the white flash of the aircrew cadet) and standard of drill, an exhilarating sensation if we completed a complicated movement successfully. I doubt if I have ever been fitter than I was when our six weeks at Torquay came to an end. We were lucky to have in charge of us intelligent and sympathetic officers and NCOs who knew how to motivate us and to keep our eyes on the stars while keeping our boots highly polished and firmly on the ground.

I also decided to attend to my spiritual health while at Torquay. My parents were not at that time church or chapel-goers. (I gathered that my father was not a great believer in the teachings of the Christian Church after his experiences in the

First World War; this did not stop him singing the more doleful hymns such as "For those in peril on the sea" which also did duty as a lullaby for his children and grandchildren). My brother and I attended Sunday School in a local Methodist Church, but it was not until after I entered the Grammar School that I discovered the Church of England and the beauty of its services in the language of the Authorised Version of the Bible and the Book of Common Prayer. With one or two friends I began attending St Paul's Church in Sketty, about a mile from my home in Ty Coch. We attended Evensong more than we did Morning Prayer since the attractions of cycling around the Gower Peninsula on a Sunday were too strong to resist. The Church was always full with a faithful congregation and my friends and I sat, by direction from the church wardens, in the last pew on the right hand side of the Church where our limited view of the Vicar did not detract from the enjoyment of services filled with good singing of hymns and psalms, eloquent reading of the Lessons and firm instruction in the sermon. But none of my parents or the clergy and laity of the Church broached with me the idea of confirmation into the Church of England. This came at Torquay where I attended Church Parade at St Luke's Church and was confirmed by the Bishop of Crediton on 10 September 1941.

In a book I read many years later it was asserted that after ITW aircrew cadets went to a Grading School for twelve hours flying instruction, after which the most promising were sent for pilot training at one of the overseas flying schools of the Empire Flying Training Scheme. That did not happen to my 49 fellow cadets and me. At the end of our six weeks in Torquay we travelled by train to Greenock on the Clyde, where we were embarked on a troopship and, as the lowest of the low by rank, were billeted deep down in the ship's decks. While we were moored in the Clyde I was impressed by the daring of the Scots boys among us, who, aided and abetted by the crew, slipped ashore overnight to visit their families. Technically absent without leave, none of them was caught and none of them missed the eventual sailing in convoy of our ship (which I think was SS Shropshire). We had been issued with tropical kit (solar topee, khaki shirts, shorts and stockings) before leaving Torquay, so we surmised that we were bound for training in Rhodesia or South Africa under the Empire Flying Training Scheme (EFTS). Some of us had to learn to sleep in hammocks while others slept on the mess tables at which we ate, read and wrote letters during the day. The food did not match the Torquay standard but I was luckier than most since I was selected to assist a signaller on the bridge, and as a reward for such duty enjoyed well-made cocoa on the bridge and a proper meal made for the officers' mess.

After an eventless six weeks at sea we arrived at Durban and enjoyed what was virtually a fortnight's holiday plus the hospitality of the English-origin Durbaners, before taking the train to Bulawayo in Rhodesia where we were accommodated in the Agricultural Show Grounds. My billet was a pig sty (all the animals had left!), which I endured for three long boring months in this so-called Initial Training Wing (at Hillside) of the Rhodesia Air Training Group, where we received no instruction beyond square bashing under the orders of foul-mouthed South African/Rhodesian accented junior NCOs. At the end of January 1942 I moved on to No. 26 Elementary Flying Training School at Guinea Fowl Air Station for elementary flying training on de Havilland Tiger Moths (two-seater fabric-covered biplanes with a de Havilland Gipsy Major engine generating 130 BHP on take-off). The delay in my call-up (from 1939 to 1941) and the further delay at Bulawayo indicated that our country was woefully short of the training facilities it required to put into the air the numbers of trained pilots required to fight an air war successfully.

Looking back on my elementary flying training I am surprised that we achieved so much in such a short time. Although I had devoured a "Teach Yourself to Fly" manual (my instructor borrowed it since, he said, it had given me a good grounding in the theory of flight), I was slow in going solo. My instructor (a First World War Royal Flying Corps pilot who between the Wars had been working in Iran for the Anglo-Persian Oil Company) insisting upon thirteen hours dual instruction before letting me complete, alone, the ritual "circuit and bump". Thereafter, and with a great sensation of relief that I had gone solo, I flew hour-long navigational exercises over Rhodesia, including night flying, and never got lost. This "map in the boot" skill was to serve me well (except once in 1944) throughout my flying career at a time when single-seater aircraft had no navigational aids to guide the pilot on his way. One incident at Guinea Fowl which could have ended my flying career was when another pupil pilot in a Tiger

Moth flew into my tailplane and rudder while we were in the circuit preparing to land. I was able to land my Tiger Moth successfully and to escape, along with the other pilot, any blame or punishment for the mishap since our instructors could not agree whether one or both of us was to blame.

The flying accident at Guinea Fowl and its happy outcome were another proof of the remarkable qualities of the Tiger Moth as a cheap, reliable and safe trainer aircraft for the Royal Air Force. It was also said that the Tiger Moth magnified the faults of the pupil pilot and was therefore a boon to his instructor and ultimately to the pupil himself, who otherwise might have gone forward to more advanced and operational flying with a fault or faults undetected and potentially fatal to himself and others. By 1945 some 9000 Tiger Moths had been manufactured and all the RAF's wartime pilots probably had their first experience of flying and learned to fly on Tiger Moths. This remarkable little aircraft is still in action today with flying clubs and private owners.

From Guinea Fowl with 66 hours flying experience on Tiger Moths (half of it dual with an instructor) I proceeded to No. 22 Senior Flying Training School at Thornhill Air Station near Gwelo. Here we were given the strange rank of Acting Sergeant Unpaid (ASU) and made members of the Sergeants' Mess. After a month or so those of us being considered for a commission were moved into the Officers' Mess. Thornhill gave us six months advanced training on North American Harvards. These were dual control low-wing monoplanes with a Pratt and Whitney Wasp Junior engine generating 300 BHP. Quite a jump from the Tiger Moth: the Harvard looked enormous when first seen on the ground; and the ground a long way below when one first sat in the cockpit, which, after the pattern of American fighters, was roomy and comfortable for the pilot. It was a particularly handy aircraft for close formation flying: one could tuck a wing behind the wing of the formation leader and achieve a neat, stable and highly satisfactory pattern eloquent of one's skill as a pilot. It was also a good aerobatic aircraft, but I failed to come up to the expectations of the examining instructor when I took my final flight with him. He kept me at aerobatics for an hour, explaining afterwards that I was so close to achieving an above average rating that he had given me an extended chance:

but Good Average was the best he could award me. When I was awarded my wings I had flown 218 hours, including 152 hours on Harvards of which 100 were solo flying.

"Awarded my wings" sounds splendid, and it was, in substance but not in form. Unlike the picture presented by wartime newsreels and films and books on the RAF, there was, at Thornhill, no magnificent parade with everyone looking his airmanlike best and a proud pilot marching up to a distinguished senior officer to have his wings pinned onto his chest. At Thornhill we ambled in single file into the office of the Commanding Officer, a Rhodesian Group Captain, who rooted around in a drawer of his desk and came up with the RAF wings insignia and a "There you are". Similarly with my commissioning as a Pilot Officer: "Better get yourself a uniform". It seemed to me that he was totally uninterested in the whole business and not the best type of Commanding Officer for a group of dedicated and encouraging instructors, who had no hesitation in saying "Congratulations! Well done!" - words that the Group Captain might have made an effort to squeeze out.

An unusual occurrence one day at Thornhill entailed the cancellation of all flying training and the despatch in formation of all the Harvards for "a show of strength", as it was described, along the frontier with Portuguese Mozambique, presumably to reassure Britain's "oldest ally" that all was well. Or perhaps it was just to break the monotonous routine of training for the instructors. Whatever the motive, everyone - instructors and pupils - felt that an additional and positive contribution had been made to the war effort.

After a visit to the Victoria Falls and a week's holiday in Salisbury, now Harare, the capital city of Rhodesia, with the two good friends Hugh Loudon and Joe Malone, both from Glasgow but from very different parts of that city, who had trained with me and shared my room and adventures (including the joint purchase for £11 of a 1928 Erskine tourer, in which we explored the "bundu"), we enjoyed a four-day train journey in comfortable sleeping cars from Salisbury to Cape Town. Of this train journey I have two outstanding memories: the beauty of moonlight on the Drakensberg Mountains, and a train stop in the middle of the "bundu" when everyone, including the crew, disembarked to enjoy a cold beer from a hut which seemed to exist for this one purpose of dispensing cold beer to passing trains. From the sublime to the ridiculous perhaps, but both events were unique in my experience.

After a short time at a transit camp in Cape Town (the early morning tea served to officers in their billets was quite horrible) and the essential trip to the top of Table Mountain, we were embarked on the SS Oronsay under orders to return to the United Kingdom and not to the Middle East, whither all the pilot drafts preceding ours had been directed. We were delighted at the prospect of returning home and also at the pleasure of a six week voyage in a comparatively empty troopship carrying only a draft of pilots and a few other military personnel also bound for Britain. We also learned that the Oronsay was not to await a convoy but was to make an unescorted solo dash for home. "Why?" we asked. "Because you chaps are needed at home," came the reply. Ours not to reason why; so we settled down to enjoy the luxury of a cabin each and privacy when we wanted it.

It was indeed a comfortable and pleasant voyage until the early morning of 9 October 1942, when the Oronsay was torpedoed by a German submarine. I was asleep in my cabin at the time and fell out of my bunk as the ship heeled over. My first thought was to retrieve my uniform, including hat, from the wardrobe. This done, I was out of my cabin and making my way on to deck with one foot on the floor and one foot on the wall. Arriving on deck I saw that the lifeboats on the port side were useless since the ship had heeled to starboard. The crew had cut away the boats on the starboard side and it was necessary to climb down a rope into a boat. Not all the passengers were as lucky as I was in making this somewhat perilous descent successfully, and many were in the water. Those of us in the boats pulled the less fortunate out of the water, reviving them where necessary. We learned later that one seaman had lost his life, a tragedy that would inevitably have been greater if, with only half the lifeboats available, the troopship had been full. I found that I had lost my uniform trousers, which must have slipped off the hanger somewhere between my cabin and the deck; but I had my uniform hat and jacket and my pyjama trousers so I was relatively well clothed.

The submarine surfaced and played its searchlight over us but made no contact and soon disappeared again under the water. So there we were, in twelve lifeboats, six hundred miles from Freetown in West Africa. The Master and First Officer of the Oronsay took command of the flotilla and decreed that we would make for Freetown, sailing with what sails we had during the heat of the day and rowing during the twelve hours of night. Food and drink was a hard biscuit, with pemmican (a beef preparation something like a coarse Gentleman's Relish) and a dipper of water, a mouthful twice a day, later reducing, so far as biscuit/pemmican was concerned, to once a day. After three days a violent storm blew up during the night, scattering the flotilla and splitting it into two parts. When dawn came we found that we could gather six boats together; there was no sign of the other six. (We learned later, after our return to Britain, that these six had also regrouped but had been picked up by the Vichy French and taken to Dakar where our comrades were given a bad time by their rescuers). Heavy rain refilled our water butts and soaked us. We sailed and rowed (I wore out the seat of my pyjamas and repaired it with sail cord) for a further five days, followed always by sharks and occasionally having to restrain one of our number who found the strain unbearable and would try to throw himself overboard. We could only hope that we would be rescued: there was no guarantee. One sad case was an older man who suddenly stood up, announced that he had to catch the next tramcar and made to step over the side. Then came the great relief of being sighted by a Royal Air Force Sunderland flying boat which found us, we also learned later, at the very middle of the square search it was making for the Oronsay or survivors. We had rowed 300 miles. We were lucky since one more change of direction by the Sunderland and he would have been on his way back to Freetown without sighting us. The next, ninth, day of our lifeboat voyage, we were picked up by HMS Brilliant, a destroyer which had been directed our way by the Sunderland. The Royal Navy, officers and men, were marvellous, making us welcome to their messes with food and drink in the quantities we could, at that stage, safely absorb. A few of the merchant seamen rescued with us showed that lack of discipline which had appeared from time to time in the lifeboats: challenging the Master's and Chief Officer's command and stealing water as the dipper was passed down the lifeboat. On the destroyer it showed up as they rolled around the deck in pain, having over-imbibed against the advice of the sailors. That was the only time I have seen men drunk on water.

In Freetown we were transferred to a ship full of survivors from ships sunk by enemy action in the South Atlantic. From Freetown to Britain in convoy provided an uneventful journey of which I have no memory except that we played a lot of unserious bridge. Back at home we were given two weeks leave and twenty pounds to reequip ourselves with uniform necessities: our other losses (for example, presents for the family and a diamond engagement ring I was bringing home for Christina) were on our own account and no concern of the Royal Air Force. This was somewhat disappointing, since the merchant seamen in our lifeboat had earlier irritated us with their endless discussion of the compensation they would receive for their ordeal and losses and what they could claim for. I had also lost my Pilot's Log Book containing the details of my flying training in Rhodesia. But we were young - I celebrated my 21st birthday on the survivor ship; I soon got rid of the scurvy sores that broke out on my face and was keen to get back to flying. On 23 November 1942 I was in the air again at the controls of a Miles Master trainer (Rolls Royce Kestrel or Pratt and Whitney Twin Row Wasp engine) at No. 5 Advanced Flying Unit (AFU) at Tern Hill in Shropshire. I am fully persuaded that we were lucky not to have experienced the "counselling" for stress, which seems such a feature of life today.

The Welsh, perhaps all the tribal people of Britain, but certainly not the detribalised inhabitants of the South East of England, have an unsophisticated, even naïve, but gentle way of bringing one down to earth. Thus when I went home for the first time proudly wearing my RAF pilot's wings, a neighbour asked me "Have you been up?"

Having completed my advanced flying course at Tern Hill five days before Christmas 1942, on 27 December I was flying

Hurricanes Mark 1 (Rolls Royce Merlin Mark III engine) from 56 Operational Training Unit (OTU) at Tealing near Dundee in Scotland. Here I learned to be a fighter pilot, spending much time on aerobatics (I perfected looping a Hurricane with the engine throttled right back: it wobbled a bit, and tried to stall at the top of the loop when we were upside down), dog fighting and air to air firing, as well as navigation, formation and high and low flying exercises designed to meet all situations in which a fighter pilot might find himself.

One predicament in which I found myself occurred after a height climb and exercise at 30,000 feet on a bitterly cold day on 4 January 1942. I did not know it, but the wheels on my Hurricane had frozen solid, with the result that when I landed it slid along the snow-covered runway until we ran out of it and slowly toppled forward onto its nose, breaking the wooden propeller but doing no other damage. The Flight Commander, a Flight Lieutenant Johnnie Johnson, magnanimously told me that I was forgiven; but he did not tell me what sin I had committed; and I did not ask! (I was to be grateful on another occasion to the wooden propeller on my Hurricane).

It was at Tealing that I first read the poem "High Flight" by John Gillespie Magee, the son of an American father and English mother who was educated at Rugby and killed in action over Britain at the age of 19 in December 1941. I have no hesitation in quoting it in full here since it is intensely evocative of the sheer joy of taking a single-seat single-engine fighter plane up high and throwing it around the sky through every manoeuvre of which pilot and plane are capable. Even today when I read the poem I relive the excitement of an experience in Hurricane and Spitfire so beautifully and humbly expressed by John Gillespie Magee.

> *Oh! I have slipped the surly bonds of earth,*
> *And danced the skies on laughter silvered wings:*
> *Sunward I've climbed, and joined the tumbling mirth*
> *Of sunlit clouds – and done a hundred things*
> *You have not dreamed of – and wheeled and*
>   *soared and swung*
> *High in the sunlit silence. Hov'ring there*

> *I've chased the shouting wind along, and flung*
> *My eager craft through footless halls of air.*
>
> *Up, up, the long delirious, burning blue!*
> *I've topped the windswept heights with easy grace*
> *Where never lark, or even eagle flew:*
> *And, while with silent, lifting mind I've trod*
> *The high untrespassed sanctity of space,*
> *Put out my hand – and touched the face of God.*

I passed out from 56 OTU with A Good Average rating as a fighter pilot and was posted immediately to 184 Squadron at Colerne near Bath where, in a christening ceremony conducted by the Squadron Commander, "Bunny" Rose, I was named "Archie", the two pilot officers who had joined with me, Anthony Charles William Fairhead and Joseph Best being given respectively the names of "Oscar" and "Joe", Bunny Rose's inventiveness failing him in the latter case. "Archie" stuck and I have been so called ever since.

184 was not a fighter squadron but an experimental unit equipped with Hurricane IID aircraft to experiment with armaments different to the eight .303 machine guns which had served the Hurricane so well in the Battle of Britain. We experimented with 40 millimetre cannon slung below the wings and rocket projectiles similarly sited and fitted with warheads of solid shot or 60 pounds of explosive. We tried various ways of sighting these new weapons on targets (eventually using a fighter gunsight turned on its side with the graticule of the sight adjusted to show 600 yards from the target) and demonstrated these weapons and the tactics to be used to parties of senior officers from Army, Navy and Air Force. We spent much of our time attacking tanks, either in simulated operations or in earnest against actual worn-out (and unmanned) vehicles. We also tried out the solid shot rocket projectiles against enemy shipping in the Channel and discovered that solid shot was ineffective, merely making a hole in the side of a vessel which the crew could quickly and easily plug. The 40 mm cannon was too inaccurate by far and we soon came to appreciate the power and accuracy of the rocket projectile with the 60 pounds of explosive in its nose.

Most of the squadron's flying was non-operational, but during a night patrol off Calais on Friday 13 August 1943, looking for an enemy ship under the direction of the flight controllers at Dover (I was operating from Manston), I received my baptism of fire. I did not find the ship, got too near to Calais and that port's anti-aircraft guns opened up on me with quick success, hitting my Hurricane Mark IV somewhere, causing it to judder violently but not sending it out of control. I returned to base where, after landing, it was discovered that the wooden propeller blades had been shot away and that I had flown the Hurricane home on the propeller stubs. A tribute to the solid construction of the Hurricane; but what would have happened if the propeller had had steel blades?

Some of our non-operational flying was also hazardous, particularly when it involved very low-level flying in unstable weather conditions to test out the cannon or rockets. On one occasion I hit overhead power cables to Betteshanger Colliery in Kent, the cables passing between the Hurricane's wings and the 40mm cannon slung below, tearing the cannon off their mountings. I had to confess to the resulting inquiry that I had not seen the cable but, since this hazard was not marked on the map I had, the simulated operation was in wooded surroundings and the exercise was authorised, I escaped any penalty. Yet again a demonstration of the strength of the Hurricane.

The squadron was forbidden to cross the enemy coast for fear that the loss of an aircraft would reveal the secrets of the rocket projectiles. But after the VI attacks began in late 1943 the squadron was authorised in December of that year to cross into France to attack the launch pads of the VI weapon in an operation named "Noball". Almost immediately I led two attacks on a reported site at Brunchaptre, one by dive-bombing with eight RPs and one at low-level, firing eight RPs from 200 yards range: the latter was far more spectacular and successful. During the second attack my aircraft was struck by enemy fire for the second time. January 1944 was a busy month for "Noball" with dive-bombing attacks on sites at Ligescourt, Tournehem and Montorgueil. It was while I was leading the squadron back across France from one of these raids that the controller at Dover called me (on my unromantic call-sign of Brownbag Leader) to warn, in his usual calm voice, of a squadron of Focke Wulf 190 fighters above us. This was not welcome news, since the Hurricane Mark IV was not a fighter. It was heavy with armour and rocket rails and had a top speed of only 180 mph. I put the squadron nose down, flying as close to the ground as possible, the FWs did not see us and we flew back home to complete my operations in Hurricanes.

184 Squadron reequipped at Detling, near Maidstone, with Typhoon Mark 1B fighter-bombers armed with four 20 millimetre Oerlikon cannon and eight 60 lb explosive head rocket projectiles. When all this firepower was loosed at once the Typhoon delivered a broadside equal to that from a light cruiser. The Typhoon was not as easy to fly as Hurricane or Spitfire. With a 2400HP Napier-Sabre sleeve valve engine and a three – later four – bladed propeller, the torque produced on take-off caused the aircraft to veer violently to the right – especially the first time one took one off. One soon learned to trim the Typhoon to port before take-off and to keep the left rudder fully depressed until airborne. Once in the air the enormous (for those days) engine and the typically clean Hawker cut of the aircraft made it a delight to fly and to employ as a weapons platform, although we did not know or use this particular piece of military jargon at that time. Perhaps I should explain that pilots of single-seat, single-engine fighter/fighter-bombers did not receive dual instruction before flying these types since, none of them was equipped with two seats. One read the pilot manual, talked over the aircraft with the Squadron or flight commander and engineer officer, and then took off to discover whether the pilot or the plane was to be in charge. It is a tribute to the thorough training we received in the RAF that the pilot usually won.

A tragic occasion happened at Detling when the pilot did lose control of his aircraft. One of our flight commanders, Flight Lieutenant Ruffhead, had obtained authority to fly a WAAF officer, Miss Pam Barton, who was the English Ladies Golf Champion, to another station in the Squadron communications aircraft, a Tiger Moth. The Tiger Moth's engine stalled on take-off, it crashed, burst into flames and Miss Barton died. The consequent Court of Inquiry exonerated Ruffhead but he was killed in action soon afterwards.

Before I finally leave the Hurricane behind at Detling, I must mention that 184 Squadron had previously been stationed at Colerne, Zeals - where the control tower is now a dwelling and where, 45 years later, Christina and I bought our present home, White Cross Lodge, although I have no recollection of the week I spent at Zeals (flying every day, as my log-book tells me I did), Eastchurch (a splendid older-type RAF Mess), Merston, Manston (a first class station with a modern Officers' Mess where I enjoyed the ritual shell egg after night operations, the civilian population of Britain making do with dried egg powder), Ashford and Newchurch. Eight different bases in under a year; I doubted then if this was an efficient use of resources and I still do. After D-Day when the Allies were advancing through Europe it was essential that the Typhoon Wings moved to keep up with the Army; but why we had to move so much in a static situation, so far as our participation in the War was concerned, was a mystery. I see from my log-book that even after we reequipped with Typhoons we moved the Squadron from Detling to Odiham, to Eastchurch, back to Odiham and to Westhampnett during March and April 1944.

The squadron's reequipment/training period with Typhoons was complete by the end of March 1944, after which I left the squadron for two weeks to marry Christina on 8 April and honeymoon at Malvern Wells. The Squadron party given by Bunny Rose and Co to celebrate my forthcoming marriage ended with myself spreadeagled on the floor while Rose painted ribald slogans on my stomach with iodine. One cannot deny that spirits of all sorts were high and plentiful after a successful conversion to Typhoons and a wedding in the Squadron.

The pace of operations now began to quicken for 184 Squadron. On 7 May the best man at my wedding, Joe Best, after a brave struggle to bring his damaged Typhoon back across the Channel, had to bale out at 800 feet to be picked up injured but safely by the Air Sea Rescue Service. Four other members of the squadron were not so lucky and were lost over France. In the run-up to D-Day we attacked woods (where intelligence had detected enemy concentrations or stores), ammunition dumps, troop billets, wireless stations, railway junctions and ship reporting stations.

On the afternoon of D-Day 184 squadron had its first engagement with German tanks, ten of them east of Caen. We claimed that we destroyed at least five of them. Our next attack on tanks in Mezidon station was not so successful: three of our number were shot down. We returned to the same target in the afternoon and were more successful this time: perhaps we had done better than we thought in the morning, since the flak that surrounded us on our second visit was not so intense as it had been during the first. On one of our missions, on 13 June, I had to put down in Normandy on one of the emergency strips which engineering commandos had laid out for such a circumstance as mine: an engine that did not wish to keep turning smoothly. The engineers found the trouble - an air lock in the petrol feed - and I flew back to base at Westhampnett. Although I had been adrift only a few hours, the squadron adjutant had reported me missing, causing unnecessary distress to Christina and to our families, and anger in me and the Squadron Commander, who considered, quite rightly, that the adjutant had jumped the gun and acted without proper authority. Bunny Rose had the adjutant posted away from the squadron, and I acted as adjutant.

The emergency strip on which I landed on 13 June was built on a wheatfield, as were all the other strips in Normandy. After the Typhoons had used these strips a few times the resultant dust was too much for the engine filters, which had to be changed. We had moved to the emergency landing strip (ELS) No. B4 at Beny-sur-mer before this happened to 184 Squadron, which spluttered its way back to Holmesley South for the necessary engineering work, which took us off operations for only two days. The speed with which the dust problem was diagnosed and the modified filter developed was a great credit to the RAF's and Hawkers' and Napier's engineers. After that I had engine problems only once, and that when I was air testing a Typhoon which had been troublesome.

On 6 July we moved the squadron to ELS B.10 at Plumetot and resumed the quick up-and-down attacks on enemy tanks and positions which were a feature of Typhoon operations in Normandy: we were close to the front line. Twenty minutes was the shortest time I was in the air for some of my sorties. On 14 July we moved to ELS B5 at La Fresne Camilly where we joined 121

Wing of 83 Group of the Second Tactical Air Force, formed to take over from Army Cooperation Command the conduct of air operations after D-Day. 83 Group was formed in 1943 as part of Fighter Command to be an important component of 2nd TAF when the latter became operational. 184 Squadron had been a member of 83 Group since the latter's formation in April 1943 and in its wanderings, which I have described above, had been attached to 122, 125 and 128 Wings of the Group, but on D-Day we were the only constituent squadron of 129 Wing. This Wing had been awarded to the Canadians to command, but their Air Force (RCAF), which served with such distinction, did not have enough squadrons to man it. The food provided by the Canadians was superb, the best I had in 2nd TAF, but perhaps they were lucky in having to cook for only one squadron, not the three or four which made up the normal Wing. The Canadian Group Captain (who did not fly in my experience of him) was a pompous fellow who reprimanded me for coming into the Mess (a marquee) wearing a rollneck sweater. I explained that I was in for a quick lunch between operations; he replied that I should always wear a collar and tie in the Mess. I had my lunch.

121 Wing, under the inspiring command of Group Captain Tim Morice, a First World War pilot who flew his Typhoon like the rest of us, was a more professional unit of four squadrons, 174, 175 and 245 in addition now to 184. On 27 July Mr Churchill visited us, flying in a captured Fieseler Storch (which could land on a sixpence) flown by Air Vice Marshal Harry Broadhurst, the Air Officer Commanding 83 Group. The AOC told us that Mr Churchill had tried to persuade him "to fly somewhere where I can see the fighting". Mr Churchill gathered us around him, mounted a box to give himself a better view of us all and showed his emotion as tears began to roll down his cheeks. He spoke: "I know you chaps are short of booze; I am never short of it, so I know how you are suffering." He could not have made a better speech. We cheered him spontaneously and willingly and voted his visit a great success. We did not give the same accolade to the Air Minister, Archibald Sinclair, who also visited us around this time. He made the fatuous remark, when examining the blackboard presentation of our triumphs and efforts: "I see that you have fired more cannon shells than rockets. Why is that?" We concluded that if the Air Minister did not know the difference between the rate of fire of four 20 millimetre cannons and

eight rockets he probably did not know much else about the conduct of war in the air. We also received a visit from Ernest Hemingway, the writer; and Frank Wootton, probably Britain's leading aviation artist, spent some time at 121 Wing painting among other pictures, his most famous depiction of Typhoons attacking German armour at Falaise. In his note to this painting, written after he had visited the battlefield, Wootton wrote inter alia "the ground was littered with burnt-out vehicles and armour, some caught nose-to-tail in deeply cut roads. The gray-clad bodies of German soldiers were everywhere. It had to be painted: the dust and smoke of battle would have prevented any photographer obtaining an overall picture". (I am lucky to own a reproduction of this painting and others by Frank Wootton in a book of his aviation art presented to me in 1980 by General Buzz Baxter of the United States Air Force, who was the Air Force Commander in NATO's Allied Forces North Headquarters in Oslo when I was British Ambassador to Norway. Buzz later became Commander in Chief of the United States Air Force in Britain before retiring to his native Texas).

The war went on, the most outstanding operations in which I was engaged being the Battle of Mortain on 7 August and of Falaise the same month. The German General von Kluge launched an attack at Mortain with six Panzer divisions in an attempt to cut off two American Army Corps and sever the communications of the United States Army in Normandy. The attack was helped by heavy mist in the morning, but at around lunchtime it cleared and the Typhoons were loosed on the enemy in low-level assaults. I led two sorties that afternoon and claimed two Tiger tanks and an armoured fighting vehicle (AFV) for myself. As I was coming in on one of the Tigers I saw his gun fire at me; fortunately he missed me but I did not return the compliment. The battle was short, swift and brutal, lasting for only about two hours before the battle area became shrouded in dust. The German attack was broken by the 294 sorties flown by the rocket-firing Typhoons of 83 Group. In his account of this battle in his book *Crusade in Europe* (1948) the Supreme Allied Commander, General Dwight D Eisenhower refers to the RAF having "a large number of Typhoons equipped with rocket firing devices. These made low-flying attacks against the enemy armour and kept up a sustained assault against his forces that was of great help to the defending infantry". (His strange reference to "rocket firing devices" suggests that the Supreme Allied Commander had not come to terms with new weaponry of the rocket projectile; but he was not so far adrift as Archibald Sinclair). Six years later when I was at the Embassy in Bucharest, I met Colonel Bobby O'Brien, the United States Military Attaché, who had been a tank commander at Mortain. He had no hesitation in greeting me as his saviour when he learned that I had been in a Typhoon at Mortain.

The Battle of the Falaise Gap (or Pocket) lasted for ten days and turned the German retreat in this area into a rout. As the German General von Luttwitz, commanding the Second Panzer Division, put it later, "the intervention of the Tactical Air Forces, especially the Typhoons, was decisive. They came down in hundreds, firing their rockets at the concentrated tanks and vehicles. We could do nothing against them".

During the Falaise operation I was promoted Flight Lieutenant and senior flight commander of 245 Squadron. I was sitting in the Mess (still a marquee) on the evening of 17 August when the C.O., Bunny Rose, came up and told me that the Group Captain, Tim Morice, wished to speak to me on the telephone. I picked up the phone and Morice's voice said: "Look here, young Lamb!" - I was 22 - "I want you to take over a flight in 245 right away. Have you got any braid? No? Well, I'll give you some. Get it sewn on right away." The time was around 9.30 pm so I did not bother about the braid that night, but when I reported to the Wing Commander, a Rhodesian named Green whom we lost during the Falaise operation, in the morning, he gave me the braid with a further injunction to get it sewn on right away. I celebrated that day, 18 August, by leading two sorties and claiming a couple of AFVs and a truck for myself.

The commander of 245 Squadron was "Skip" Zweigbergk, British despite his name of Dutch origin, a large man with a large sense of humour and a large capacity for leadership of the best sort, in the air and on the ground. My fellow flight commander was Harry Bathurst and the three of us plus four other members of the squadron were awarded DFCs by the end of 1944. But we also lost some good fellows. My elevation in rank was also marked by a classier and more appropriate call-sign: Archduke, in place of the Brownbag of 184 Squadron. 245 was called (in brackets) the Northern Rhodesia Squadron, dedicated to that colonial territory in recognition of funds raised there for the war effort. There were never any Rhodesians, North or South, in the Squadron but we had some splendid Canadians and Australians (always pretending to be "bolshie"), a New Zealander and a South African in addition to the British who made up most of our complement. This was twelve pilots per flight plus the Squadron Commander, twenty-five in all with eighteen aircraft. The CO and the flight commanders appropriated an aircraft each for themselves with the other twenty-two pilots sharing the remaining fifteen. The system worked well since we normally flew eight aircraft at a time in two lots of four in a sortie. This arrangement also gave the ground crew, who worked dedicatedly to keep our aircraft serviceable, enough time to do their work always to the high standard they inevitably achieved. A ground crew team of seven (engineers, fitters, riggers, armourers, radio technicians) was required to keep a Typhoon and its pilot happy to fly.

On 28 August we made our first move forward to keep up with the Army, relocating ourselves at ELS B24 at St André de L'Eure. I completed my August operations with an attack on a German transport column east of Amiens. The unusual feature of this attack was that it involved firing on horse-drawn transport.

The Army was now advancing fast, and between 2 and 4 September we moved from St André to Beauvais and from Beauvais to Douai. The weather was bad - we had to turn back on our first attempt to fly from St André to Beauvais - and I failed to distinguish myself by getting myself lost and having to land at Poix on my way to Douai. We now turned our attention to shipping in the Scheldt before moving to Antwerp on 17 September, the day the Allies launched their airborne assault on Arnhem. 83 Group was committed to supporting the Army advance from the south to relieve the airborne formations. It was a frustrating experience. At the end of the first day the army sent us a message of thanks for our help; but for the next three days the weather was extremely bad, with visibility at ground level so poor that very little effective support could be given to the Army. I managed four attacks on German positions in direct support of the troops at Arnhem, one of which, although successful in silencing some German guns, was carried out in a mêlée of attacking Typhoons, Allied medium bombers, intercepting Luftwaffe fighters and intense flak.

In our advance out of Normandy we had attacked enemy river craft on the Seine; we now carried out similar attacks on the Rhine and attacks on railway movements - "train-busting" - in North Holland, even though the weather remained "pro-Nazi" as I noted it in my log book. 83 Group was allocated a tactical area north and north east of the Rhine in which to disrupt movement as much as possible. We also had a new enemy to contend with, the jet-propelled ME262, which was first sighted on 9 September. It was not a real menace since there were so few of them and their range was so small, but Group decided that we should try to destroy them on their own airfields at Rheine. Thus 121 Wing was given the opportunity of a full wing attack by its four squadrons on a Rheine base. I led 245 Squadron as the fourth squadron to attack, which meant that the sky was well-filled with flak when we dived but also that I could see that the Wing Commander, Pitt-Brown, had led a successful attack. (I met Pitt-Brown again in the 1970s when he was a businessman working temporarily in Kuwait and I was British Ambassador there. This was an exceptional meeting since, perhaps because of my overseas service as a diplomat, my path did not cross those of former RAF colleagues. The only other such meeting I had was at Victoria Station in the 1960s with "Dutch" Holland who had been shot down at Mezidon as I have described earlier).

Another sortie I led on 16 October got me a mention in the newspapers. I quote from the *South Wales Evening Post* of 17 October:

> *Flight Lieutenant Archie Lamb, of London and Swansea, led a successful attack by rocket Typhoons on a battery of German field guns near Vernay (sic: it should have been Venreij).*
>
> *The battery, which had been giving much trouble to Second Army formations, was attacked on the call of our forward troops and, flying through*

> *cloud and mist and bad flying weather, a Typhoon formation poured 56 rockets and many cannon shells into the position.*
>
> *After a direct rocket hit on one of the big guns the position blew up.*
>
> *After the attack there were two clouds of smoke rising from the target area and many small explosions were seen.*

This account, presumably written by a Group public relations man after our debriefing and information from the Army, who sent me a message of thanks and congratulations, gives a succinct account of the close support which the Typhoons were able to give the Army. We navigated by a one inch to the mile map (carried in the left boot) on which we were able to mark accurately, "pin-point", the enemy target over which the Army would fire red smoke shells as we approached. "Achtung! Typhoon!" became one of the most frightening alerts for the German soldier, who never gave up and who hit my Typhoon for the third time over Arnhem. I was leading the squadron at 8,000 feet preparatory to diving when a burst of 88-millimetre anti-aircraft fire bracketed my aircraft. My No. 2 enquired if I was all right; I asked him to have a look around my Typhoon; he reported that he could see no damage so we flew on to attack. On returning to base my rigger pointed out that shrapnel had hit the fuselage just behind the cockpit at head height but had caused no serious damage.

I have mentioned above that the squadron was at 8000 feet preparing to dive. Before such a dive the command was given to form echelon formation to starboard (to the right). I always found the sight of the other aircraft of the squadron in perfect formation to my right, each one stepped slightly higher than the one nearer to me, an exhilarating and heart-warming sight. Before I led the Squadron in a dive from 8000 feet, I first let the target come along the port side into the junction between the wing and the fuselage. As the target disappeared under the wing I rolled the Typhoon to port onto its back and pulled the control column tight into my stomach. This manoeuvre would give me, and the Squadron, the steepest dive possible with the target immediately in front of us. We fired our rockets at 2000 feet (in a low level attack it would be at 600 yards) and then pulled out of the dive, which caused us to black out (lose consciousness) and recover again between six and eight thousand feet. We would have been diving at around 550 mph when we pulled out. I always tried to lead an attack from behind the enemy line, normally from east to west, so that when my pilots pulled up they were facing home and would have a better chance of coming down in allied territory if they got into trouble.

121 Wing had now moved from Antwerp to a former Luftwaffe airfield at Volkel in Holland; but before leaving Antwerp I had received a letter from Christina announcing that she was expecting our first child, who was born, a daughter Elizabeth, on 12 April 1945. While I was reading Christina's letter to the background of Frank Sinatra singing "Long ago and far away" on one of the two playable records remaining for the squadron gramophone, the Germans began some desultory mortaring of the airfield. But I could not stop myself taking a walk around the airfield in celebration of the news from Christina.

Volkel was bleak and the weather in November 1944 was poor with wet or snowbound airfields making it difficult for 83 Group to operate. Fortunately the Army was consolidating and little close support was required. But my last two operational sorties on 18 and 19 November were in close support against enemy strong points in a brickworks near Roermond and in the German village of Beek. For both these attacks I received "Thank you" signals from the Army. On 6 December Wing Commander Pitt-Brown told me that I was to be rested from operations. I had flown 106 operational sorties totalling 108 hours of operational flying and that, he said, was enough.

After Christmas at home with Christina, when we discovered the magical properties of RAF uniform, wings and a DFC to extract favours from shopkeepers from under the counter, and we did not refuse any reasonable offer, I was posted as an instructor on the operational tactics of Typhoons to 55 Operational Training Unit at Aston Down in Gloucestershire. This was a beautiful place in lovely countryside with a task that was far from onerous. The joy of flying Typhoons in peaceful conditions did not detract from the serious intent of instructing pilots in their operational role. The war in Europe ended on 8 May 1945 and on 27 May we taxied our beloved Typhoons into a field adjoining Aston Down airfield and abandoned them: a sad sight. By September of that year all the Typhoons in Second Tactical Air Force had been withdrawn and all Typhoons in the RAF were scrapped by 1947. Only one remained and is now in the RAF Museum at Hendon.

My next posting was to no. 3 Glider Instruction School at Culmhead near Taunton where I enjoyed the fun of flying Hotspur two-seater gliders and was instructed in towing them aloft. My next posting was to No. 5 Glider Towing School at Shobdon, near Presteigne in Radnorshire. Christina and I found lodgings in Knighton and set up home there with our three months old daughter. Shobdon seemed to me to do the same as Culmhead; at both the general idea seemed to be that the invasion of Japan would be largely airborne and thousands of glider pilots and tug pilots would be required. Along with many of my contemporaries I was pleased and relieved when the Americans dropped an atomic bomb on Hiroshima on 6 August 1945 and the Far East War also ended. I stayed on at Shobdon until the end of October when my flying career ended. My final posting in the RAF was to the RAF Station at Membury near Newbury in Berkshire, a Transport Command Station where I was Adjutant. Being a natural bureaucrat I enjoyed this job, so much so that we never had any courts-martial. Crimes, serious in RAF terms, were referred by Group HQ to Courts of Inquiry leading to papers for a court-martial being sent to Membury. I always found something wrong with them and sent them back to Group. This pleased the Group Captain commanding Membury so much that he tried to persuade me to apply for a permanent commission in the RAF. When I went to say good-bye to him the day before my demobilisation at the end of June 1946, he showed me that he had all the necessary papers ready and invited me to sign on the dotted line there and then. I thanked him and told him, again, that I had decided to return to the Foreign Office. "God damn you, Archie," he cried. "Go and be a satellite of the State Department!" - an overstatement perhaps, but I could see what he meant.

3

Foreign Office, Rome and Genoa

I returned to the Foreign Office in July 1946 and took up the job of Registry filing clerk where I had left it in 1941. I was soon given charge of a Section and before long took over, but without promotion, a Division of the Registry serving the Information Departments. I had now reached a state where, *mirabile dictu*, I was permitted to take letters for signature to the appropriate official in the department. I remember a sympathetic diplomat, the only one to do so, expressing horror that I should have returned from the War to this. But I reckoned on not having to be patient for long since I was reasonably certain that the pre-war pattern of advancement for Foreign Office Registry clerks would be resumed, even if the promises of the 1943 Foreign Service Reform Act (the Eden/Bevin reforms) were not implemented.

It is a brave reflection of the mood of Government, Parliament and people at the height of the Second World War that an Act should be passed in 1943 radically to reform the Foreign Office, Diplomatic Service, Commercial Diplomatic Service and the Consular Services, together with their clerical and secretarial support. The White Paper (Cmd.6420 of January 1943) explained the theory and practice of an integrated Foreign Service which, it was intended, would be more efficient in carrying out the foreign policy of His Majesty's Government. The Foreign Service was to be unified in 15 Grades, from Grade A1 for the Permanent Under-Secretary and some senior Ambassadors down to Grade B6 for the Clerical Officers. The Secretarial Staff were to have their own grading. Perhaps the principal reason why the Government brought in these reforms during the War was that, first, Britain was peculiarly egalitarian and socially cohesive at that time.

Secondly, the Government wished to meet the criticism that the Diplomatic Service had been recruited from too small a circle, that it tended to represent the interests of certain sections of the nation rather than those of the country as a whole, that its members led too sheltered a life, that they had insufficient understanding of economic and social questions and that the extent of their experience was too small to enable them fully to understand the problems before them. But the Foreign Office and Diplomatic Service, which must be lumped together in pre-war terms, was only one part of the whole in so far as the conduct of Britain's overseas affairs was concerned. The criticism could not apply to the Commercial Diplomatic Service, which was recruited separately under the Department of Overseas Trade, nor to the Consular Service, who had their own recruitment procedures and their feet firmly on the ground in their dealings with the problems that human beings can run into in pursuing their interests in foreign countries. A satirical picture of the pre-1939 Diplomatic service is given by Patrick Barrington (Viscount Barrington) who, after education at Eton and Oxford, spent some years as an Honorary Attaché at the Embassy in Berlin and in the Foreign Office in London. In his poem, *Platypus*, he says:

"I had a duck-billed platypus when I was up at Trinity,
With whom I soon discovered a remarkable affinity.
He used to live in Lodgings with myself and Arthur Purvis,
And we all went up together for Diplomatic Service.
I had a certain confidence, I own, in his ability;
He mastered all the subjects with remarkable facility;
And Purvis, though more dubious, agreed that
                                   he was clever,
But no one else imagined he had any chance whatever.

I failed to pass the interview. The Board with wry grimaces
Objected to my boots and took exception to my braces;
And Purvis too was failed by an intolerant examiner,
Who said he had his doubts as to his sock-suspenders'
                                        stamina.
Our summary rejection, though we took it with urbanity,
Was naturally wounding in some measure to our vanity.
The bitterness of failure was considerably mollified,
However, by the ease with which our platypus
                                had qualified.

The wisdom of the choice, it soon appeared, was undeniable.
There never was a diplomat more thoroughly reliable,
The creature never acted with undue precipitation O,
But gave to every question his mature consideration O,
He never made rash statements that his enemies
                                  might hold him to;
He never stated anything, for no one ever told him to;
And soon he was appointed, so correct was his behaviour,
Our Minister (without portfolio) in trans-Moravia.

My friend was loved and honoured from the
                                  Andes to Esthonia;
He soon achieved a pact between Peru and Patagonia;
He never vexed the Russians or offended the Rumanians;
He pacified the Letts and he appeased the Lithuanians.
No Minister had ever worked more cautiously or slowly O;
In fact they had decided to award him a portfolio,
When, on the anniversary of Greek Emancipation,
Alas! He laid an egg in the Bulgarian Legation.

This unexpected action caused unheard-of inconvenience.
A breach at once occurred between the Turks
                                  and the Armenians;
The Greeks poured ultimata, quite unhinged by
                                  the mishap, at him;
The Poles began to threaten and the Finns began
                                  to flap at him;
The Swedes withdrew entirely from the Anglo-Saxon dailies
The right of photographing the Aurora Borealis;
And all attempts to come to a rapprochement
                                  proving barren,
The Japanese in self-defence annexed the Isle of Arran.

My platypus, once thought to be more cautious and
                                  more tentative
Than any other living diplomatic representative,
Was now a sort of warning to all diplomatic students,
The perfect incarnation of the perils of imprudence.
Beset and persecuted by the forces of reaction O,
He reaped the consequences of his ill-considered action O;
And, branded in the Honours List as Platypus, Dame Vera,
Retired, a lonely figure, to lay eggs at Bordighera."

The impact of the 1943 Act on my future as a Clerical Officer was that, if I wished (and not all my clerical colleagues did so wish) I could transfer from the Home Civil Service to the new Foreign Service in Grade B6. But before the reforms were implemented the pre-war pattern, which I expected my career to follow, took shape. In March 1947 I was promoted to Higher Clerical Officer and posted as Archivist to the Embassy in Rome with a salary of £400 a year and an annual local allowance in the same amount. Because the Embassy had been bombed out of its premises at Porta Pia by Jewish terrorists, it had been given an Administration Officer to attend to the complications of moving the Embassy to the Villa Wolkonsky. Although the move had been completed, and there was really no need for an Administration Officer, when the temporary incumbent of the post returned to London, the Higher Executive Officer who had been Archivist and de facto Administration Officer under the pre-1948 arrangements, moved exclusively into the latter role and left the Registry with its ten clerks (one of them the sister of Donald Maclean) and the Cypher Room of three clerks to me. (Many years later, as the wheel turned, or was re-invented, the Foreign Office decreed that an Embassy's Administration Officer should supervise the Registry. This was difficult, if not impossible for him [or her] to do, since he would be located away from the Registry. It would have been more sensible to have returned the administrative task to the Archivist and allowed him to attend to that side of his work while supervising his registry clerks from his desk in the Registry).

In 1947 the Embassy was still in a pre-war mode. The Ambassador, Sir Noel Charles, worked in his Residence in the Villa Wolkonsky across the garden from the Chancery, which he never visited. In the Chancery sat a Counsellor (described to me by John - later Sir John - Ward who occupied the post in 1947 as "the fifth wheel on the coach"), a First Secretary Head of Chancery, three Third Secretaries (none of whom completed a career in the Diplomatic Service) and three Honorary Attachés. These latter were wealthy young men who had no need to earn their living but found it congenial to have themselves attached to an Embassy for such duties (mostly social) as the Head of Mission might require of them. Honorary Attachés were a feature of pre-war diplomatic life but have now disappeared. The Counsellor and the Chancery had to progress to the Residence singly or in such numbers as were required by the matters submitted for His Excellency's consideration. (At this time Heads of Mission were still referred to as "H.E." by their staff; by the time I became one of Her Majesty's Ambassadors "HMA" was thankfully in use: what sane man could accept his staff, British subjects of a constitutional monarch reigning over a parliamentary democracy, referring to him as "Excellency"? The Americans refer sensibly to their Head of Mission as "Mr Ambassador"; but other foreigners and the representatives of the newer republics, whether within or without the Commonwealth, revel in the joy of Excellency).

The attitude of the diplomatic hierarchy of the Embassy towards the junior staff was the same as that I had learned to accept in the pre-war Foreign Office: "us" and "them". It was exemplified by my not being conducted across the garden into the Residence to be introduced to the Ambassador until three months after my arrival in his Embassy. When I told this story to Frank Judd, then Minister of State in the FCO, when my wife and I dined with him and Mrs Judd in 1977 shortly before I became our Ambassador to Norway, I added that in Oslo I would meet all my staff the first day I arrived. "And they'll wish to God they had not met you for three months!" Frank retorted. To complete the picture I retain of Noel Charles in his Residence, he had that day a gouty foot wrapped in bandages in the classical way on a stool before his chair. I never entered that hallowed room or saw him or exchanged a word with him again.

Noel Charles was succeeded by Sir Victor Mallet, a different type of man, who worked in the Chancery and had a kind and interested word for everybody. Ambassadors' wives were also more prominent and demanding then than they are these days (if they are sensible they will not try to emulate some Ambassadors' wives who have been under the impression that because they are married to Her Majesty's Ambassador their status is akin to that of The Queen). Lady Charles was childless and always immaculately dressed, according to Christina, who, on rare occasions, was summoned to a tea party with instructions to wear hat and gloves and an indication not to speak until spoken to. Lady Mallet, mother of a young family with one very young child with her in Rome, was warm and involved like her husband. One of Victor Mallet's delights was to lead the conga around the hallowed halls of the Villa Wolkonsky at his annual Christmas party for the Embassy staff. The Charleses never gave such a party.

Christina, Elizabeth and I had to spend three months in the Pensione Jaccarino, since in those days Embassies did not provide accommodation for their staff who had to find their own. This was not easy in post-war Rome since accommodation was scarce and the rent allowances for junior staff inadequate. Eventually we rented half a flat in the Piazza Fiume, owned and lived in (in the other half) by Avvocato Spani and his English wife. The Avvocato was a shadowy figure but the Signora had the annoying habit of inspecting our half of the flat while we were out. Our son, Robin, now Deputy Chief of Mission at our Embassy in Kuwait and one of the Service's leading Arabists, was born there on 25 November 1948. Soon after Robin's birth we were able to obtain far more comfortable and attractive accommodation in the Villa Ceccotti on the Via Cassia north of Rome in the middle of a flower garden cultivated commercially by the Ceccotti family. The Ceccotti family, who, like all Italians, seem to have an inexhaustible fund of love and tolerance for children, soon made our children favourites. When the time came for us to leave Rome and the Villa Ceccotti, the two small Ceccotti boys wept buckets at losing their playmate, Elizabeth, who remained British, dry-eyed and apparently unaffected by the touching scene.

Christina and I and our young family were lucky to have three years in Rome until 1950. The climate was equable, the shops full of good food and other items still unobtainable or in short supply in Britain; and Ostia Antica and the Roman Lakes available for weekend excursions with Amalfi in the Sorrento Peninsula our favourite resort for holidays at the Albergo Luna Convento. Unfortunately the Albergo became famous and popular and too expensive for our pocket after Roberto Rossellini and Ingrid Bergman had their love affair there in the bedroom we usually occupied.

We both learned Italian, but not so well as Elizabeth who, instructed by our Italian tuttofare, Domenica, with whom she spent a holiday in Domenica's village, spoke by her fifth birthday fluent Romano, including words that we preferred not to know.

Robin was two years old by the time we left Italy and a little confused between English and Italian, frequently using an Italian construction for his attempt at an English phrase, such as "have it a laugh". I passed a Foreign Office Italian examination and was awarded a language allowance of £30 a year. I was also assigned to Branch B of the Foreign Service, initially in Grade 5A to match my Higher Clerical Officer rank, but soon after in Grade 5, equivalent to Executive Officer in the Home Civil Service.

I acted as Administration Officer of the Embassy for three months during an interregnum between AOs. I combined this task with that of Archivist, found it less than onerous, and handed it over with reluctance to the new, inexperienced incumbent of the post. I also took over, from a Chancery diplomat, the reading of the Italian Official Gazette, translating items of interest, and continued my political education through thorough reading of the Chancery files. But what I regard as my first "diplomatic" act occurred one Sunday morning in 1948 when the Counsellor, John Ward, telephoned me to come into the Chancery immediately. He showed me a telegram from the Foreign Office and asked me to turn its substance into a Note Verbale for the Foreign Ministry, type it myself, not show it to anyone else for 48 hours, and to deliver it to the Foreign Minister, Count Sforza, with whom he had already spoken and who was awaiting me at the Palazzo Chigi. I did as I was told: the Note Verbale informed the Italian Government of the (first) devaluation of sterling.

In March 1950 I was transferred to Genoa as a supernumerary Vice-Consul to learn Consular work. There was another junior Vice-Consul beside myself and much of our time was spent standing (we were not permitted to sit) behind the Consular counter dealing with the public, British, Italian and any foreigner who required a visa for Britain or one of its colonies. We also acted for the Commonwealth countries that did not have consular representation in Genoa. I learned how to issue and endorse passports, issue visas, deal with distressed British subjects, conduct Consular marriages and handle shipping work, which was then extensive and demanding before the decline of the British merchant fleet and the amendment, almost repeal, of the Merchant Shipping Act which was our bible. Occasionally there would be a disturbance, usually caused by seamen, in the Consulate; I have never seen one sorted out so fast as by the Consul-General, Harold Swan, then approaching his 60th birthday and standing five foot nothing in his socks. I remember, too, the noble gentleman who asked me if I was a man of the world before telling me that he was on holiday with a lady who was not his wife and that they had lost their passports. He was relieved that I could help him with separate travel documents but peeved that I would not advance him funds for a continuation of his Italian Riviera idyll. Harold Swan (whose unmarried daughters were referred to inevitably as "the Cygnets") was succeeded by Consul General Fowler, who stood four foot eleven in his socks, enabling Harold to say in his farewell speech: "Whatever you may say about me, you must agree that my successor is a little Fowler."

4

Bucharest

We were in Genoa for four months before I received instructions to proceed to Bucharest as Administration Officer and Head of the Consular Section. We stayed on for a further two months in the hope that our Roumanian entry visas would come through and enable us to travel. But the Roumanian authorities were not obliging (they never were) and eventually we took a holiday at home before the issue of the visas enabled us to leave Genoa by train on 22 October to join the Arlberg Express at Basle and to arrive in Bucharest on 25 October 1950. Personnel for Bucharest always travelled in the company of the King's (now Queen's) Messengers for security reasons. The express had a restaurant car until Vienna, after which one made do as best one could in one's sleeping compartment. Here the King's Messengers came into their own: experienced in travel, they were able to conjure up dishes during the two days after Vienna which outdid, and fortified, the humble efforts of others, with eggs boiled on Tommy Cookers (of solid methylated spirit) bought at the Army and Navy Stores. Travel arrangements for Eastern Europe were far from easy. I have already mentioned the delay in obtaining Roumanian entry visas. I see from my files that we were also armed with a Hungarian transit visa, an Austrian military permit, a grey card for Vienna (I wonder what that was?), sleeper bulletins (with instructions to change sleepers at Vienna), rail tickets and meal tickets to Vienna, plus, of course, passports.

I was pleased that the task of Administration Officer had been combined with that of Consul since my experience in Rome did not suggest that the AOs job would occupy me full-time. I had, however, expressed to the Personnel Department of the Foreign Office my disappointment that I was not to be promoted to the B4 rank (Higher Executive Officer) enjoyed by my predecessor. The reply was that the Legation was being reduced in size and there would not be so much work in future. This bland reasoning was soon proved wrong by the difficulties which the Communist regime put in the way of every diplomatic, commercial, consular and administrative activity, and by the need to evacuate the remaining British subjects living in penury in Roumania. In January 1952 I was made an Acting B4 and received the pay of this grade. Meanwhile, I had become the principal Legation interlocutor with the Ministry of Foreign Affairs and the Bureau for Services to the Diplomatic Corps ("Burobin") on matters consular and administrative. Every requirement had to be argued for patiently and persistently with an educated French-speaking presence in the Ministry and a less affable ("I speak only Roumanian or Russian") gentleman (not quite the right word) in the Burobin. At the Ministry, Caius Frantescu, son of the Professor of Classics at Bucharest University, was my opponent throughout my three years in Bucharest. A silent comrade who sat in the corner and listened, to Frantescu as much as to me, I am sure, always accompanied him. Frantescu attended our farewell drinks party accompanied by his silent comrade. When they took their leave the latter spoke in English, "Don't forget us, Mr Lamb. We've had some good battles, haven't we?" I also used to see Frantescu occasionally marching in some "spontaneous" political demonstration, wearing his worker's cap and looking somewhat out of place. I hope he survived the turmoil through which the Roumanians have had to live.

An extra-curricular task which I took on was as lay reader in the English Church in Bucharest. I suppose it was apt that a Consul responsible for the temporal well-being of the British Community should also be mindful of the spiritual peace of the Anglican Congregation. Very occasionally I was successful in persuading the Roumanian authorities to grant an entry visa to the Reverend William Masters, who was officially Chaplain to the British Legation but was resident in Vienna where he ministered to the Anglican Community. We had to describe him in the visa application form as a "clerk" which was, of course, strictly true, and not as a priest, a calling that the authorities did not recognise. Apart from the priority of ministering to the Anglican Congregation, it was important to keep the English Church open and in use. Morning Prayer was said every Sunday, frequently in the presence of easily recognised security police, who were a particular worry to our Roumanian organist and his mother who bravely never missed a service, including the memorial service for King George VI following his death in 1952. I was and remain convinced that the Anglican Congregation did more than meet their own spiritual needs by keeping open their Church; they bore witness to the Roumanians, Party members, Security police and the downtrodden citizens that the strength of the Christian faith was enduring among the free people of the Western democracies.

During our three years in Roumania the people were in the grip of a Communist Police State, which had a policy of pushing the people down and down, keeping supplies of food and other goods off the market, and neglecting the maintenance of the country's infrastructure. The State also had an inexhaustible appetite for arrests and disappearances, including at least three members of the Legation local staff and two of the three doctors who were willing to take patients from the diplomatic corps. Burobin provided the servants we had and we accepted that these unfortunates would have to inform on us to save their own skins and livelihoods. We were followed wherever we went (a single Diplomatic Country Club helped the authorities to keep an eye on our recreation) and on the occasions when I had been summoned late in the evening to the Ministry Christina would be subjected to heavy breathing on the telephone. She was also followed one day, when she had collected our private mail from the Embassy, by a security policeman who came close enough to look over her shoulder at what she was carrying. The Legation had retained a villa in the Carpathian Mountains at Sinaia where the staff could, by turns, spend a weekend in beautiful surroundings, since Roumania has been well-endowed by nature. Visitors also enjoyed the company, in the basement, of Maria, the housekeeper who sang hymns and kept turkeys, which shared the basement with her. Roumania was a sad place, bearing no resemblance to the romantic Ruritanian Paris of the East, which it was said to have been, pre-war. The one joke I remember, told by a barber in the Athenee Palace Hotel, was that Russia had bred a new animal, a cross between a giraffe and a cow, so that it could be fed in Roumania and milked in the Soviet Union.

The Western Diplomatic Corps lived in a kind of ghetto, cut off not only from the people of Roumania but also from the

Missions of the Sino-Soviet Bloc. The Roumanian Government were shameless in enforcing this divide, which was made manifest at official receptions to which they had no option but to invite representatives from East and West: there would be one reception room for the former and another for the latter. If there was only one room a corridor would have been contrived down the middle. I remember one occasion when our Military Attaché, Colonel John Stevens, espied the Foreign Minister, Anna Pauker, across the divide searching in her handbag for a light for her cigarette. John crossed the divide to offer her a light, only to have his offer refused as she turned her back on him. The Western Corps always saw off, at Bucharest railway station, any of their number who were leaving. John Stevens was again prominent at these occasions as he blew his hunting horn in salute. When Tito of Yugoslavia broke with Stalin, our Yugoslav colleagues crossed the divide and became very active members of the Country Club. They also showed us in their Embassy the holes in the walls where they had detected Roumanian microphones; but they never showed us any of these microphones. They were very keen on entertaining members of the Club to folk-dancing, in which we all enjoyed a Roumanian version called the "peronitsa". This consisted of the gentlemen (one at a time) in the middle of a circle of dancers twirling a kerchief, putting it around the neck of one of the lady dancers, drawing her into the centre of the circle and, both of them kneeling on cushions, giving her a kiss. Other amusements at the club were Sunday lunches, tennis, and golf on a nine-hole course (the Roumanian authorities having confiscated the other nine for the Stalin Park of Rest and Culture). Thus, together with our retreat at Sinaia, we kept ourselves sane amid the madness of a Communist (or Socialist, as it called itself) regime which consumed its own as well as the people, Ministers and Party officials disappearing, to reappear, perhaps, in show trials. And yet there was always another Party hopeful willing to take their place and risk his neck.

We were fortunate to have as our Head of Mission Sir Walter Roberts, who was followed by Sir William Sullivan. Sir Walter and Lady Roberts welcomed us to stay in their Residence until we could move into a flat of our own (when Burobin provided it) and made us and our two small children feel quite at home. William Sullivan had a strong resemblance to Winston

Churchill and enhanced it by wearing a style of hat sometimes worn by the Great Man. So attired he arrived in Bucharest and started a rumour in the town that Churchill had arrived, suggesting that the downtrodden Roumanians would grasp at any straw which might lift them from their depression. Sullivan was extremely fond of cats, calling his somewhat timid wife Kitty, and studied the ways of ants in specially made glass containers. One day he dropped a container and the ants took the opportunity to explore every nook and cranny of the Minister's Residence. He would take me with him to drink beer in one of the far from salubrious beer halls of Bucharest to prove his theory that the British Minister could go anywhere. But he never risked the less than perfect comforts of the villa at Sinaia. Both these excellent men had come from the Consular Service – Sullivan had been known as the Red Consul in Barcelona during the Spanish Civil War – and provided, as did Harold Swan, proof of the classless commonsense of that Service.

We had our first experience of separation from our children at Bucharest. Christina had been teaching Elizabeth herself, with the help of courses provided by the Parents National Educational Union (PNEU), which provided an essential service for mothers and children when Britain's Empire was far flung, there being no schools available, but when Elizabeth was seven we decided that it would be better for her if she enjoyed the companionship and competition of other children, of whom there were few in the Western Diplomatic Corps. We sent her home to stay with an aunt and uncle, to whom we shall be ever grateful for the continual and unstinting help and affection they gave to our children whenever called upon while we were abroad. Elizabeth attended a day school near her aunt's home and had a useful and happy year there until we moved back to London in 1953.

We left Bucharest the day Stalin died to experience an eerie sort of journey of uncertainty on the part of Roumanian and Hungarian frontier officials and security policemen. Every stop of the train appeared to be cloaked in silence, everything seemed hushed, as if the people of Eastern Europe were holding their breath until they discovered whether Stalin's repressive and frightening policies would continue or be relaxed with a more friendly attitude to one and all. They soon learned that there was to be no change, none indeed for thirty years, a European generation, until the advent of Mr Gorbachev and his policies of glasnost and perestroika. Except for the unfortunate Roumanians, who continued under a native tyranny of their own which ignored the more open spirit prevailing elsewhere in their part of the continent. I must admit that when I visited Bucharest in 1968 to inspect the Embassy, there did appear to be a lightening of the atmosphere with people holding their heads up more than they did in the early 1950s; but the Ceaucescu Family soon put a stop to that. The inoculation against Marxism I experienced, during three years of seeing it in practice in Roumania, "took" and has remained valid ever since.

I have referred to the Mission in Bucharest as being both a Legation and an Embassy. It was the former and is now the latter. Before World War Two there were relatively few Embassies with Ambassadors at their head, these being in the greater powers; the lesser powers received Ministers in Legations. American foreign policy during and after the War involved sending Embassies to every country they recognised, thereby debasing the Embassy currency and forcing Britain and other European countries to follow suit and "upgrade" their Legations to Embassies.

I was made a Member of the Most Excellent Order of the British Empire (MBE) for my work in Bucharest, which included persuading the Roumanian authorities to permit forty elderly and distressed British subjects to leave for better care in their own country. While pleased with the award I thought it a pity that it took precedence over my DFC, of which, even now when I have received four decorations, I remain the most proud. My MBE also gave me the honour of being presented with the insignia by The Queen at Buckingham Palace. This made up for the disappointment of receiving my DFC through the post in 1945 and somewhat mollified my father who had been very angry in 1945 at what he regarded as "the insult".

5

Foreign Office

I returned to the Foreign Office to a post in the Recruitment and Training Section of Personnel Department. The Head of Department, Robin Hooper (DSO DFC who flew British agents into France in Lysander aircraft during the war) asked me to work out a training pattern for "hard" languages (roughly the non-Western European languages). The world had been in turmoil since the War and none of the national diplomatic services had settled down, having to move their personnel here and there to cope with crises and wars (e.g. the Russian blockade of Berlin 1948-49 and the Korean War from 1950-53). The FO had decided that it must get a grip on its language training for the new, unified Foreign Service. I began researching into the demand for language specialists and soon discovered that the Foreign Office had no information on the demand in the pre-war Diplomatic Service. The Consular Service was, however, well provided with statistics, including the important one of wastage: over a forty year career twenty percent would fall by the wayside. Sir Alexander Hutcheon was then Head of the Consular Service and was of immense help to me in drafting a pattern of supply and demand for the "hard" languages. I discovered that the greatest demand was for Arabic and that the Consular statistics suggested that wastage in the Arab World was particularly high. I found this interesting, and took myself off to the London School of Oriental and African Studies for evening classes in Arabic to discover what it was all about. My lessons and reading suggested to me that I might enjoy specialising in Arab affairs and eventually in 1955, when John Henniker-Major (MC: he jumped into Yugoslavia as a member of Fitzroy Maclean's Military Mission to Marshal Tito), who had succeeded Robin Hooper, asked me where I would like to go next I told him of my interest. John told me to post myself to the Middle East Centre for Arabic Studies (MECAS), of which more later. Meanwhile the London administrative end of MECAS was on my desk and I became involved in recruiting a new Chief Instructor for the Centre. Eventually we settled on James Craig, a lecturer in Arabic at Durham, who accepted the post, was soon seduced away from the academic world to the front-line of diplomacy, and eventually retired from the Embassy to Saudi Arabia as Sir James Craig GCMG.

I also interviewed potential candidates for the Foreign Service and was the first point of contact for successful candidates for Branch A (the Senior Branch) of the Service after they had obtained (at least) a Second Class Honours degree and passed the further tests and interviews conducted by the Civil Service Commissioners. I had gone through these tests myself in 1949 when the Foreign Office had decided that I and one other junior member of the Service should be put in for the Branch A examination. We both failed, the Commissioners giving us a marking immediately below the pass mark. I was not sure then, and am still not sure, whether the yardstick for candidates who had at least a Second Class Honours Degree was appropriate for my junior colleague and myself. Our backgrounds could not have been more different to the candidates straight down from University. But I was grateful to the Office for giving me the chance and reinforcing my confidence that I could look forward to a career in the Foreign Service.

Of all the potential candidates with whom I discussed the advantages of a diplomatic career I remember one young man. I had told him that as a member of the Foreign Service the world would be his oyster; he replied that Mummy would not want him to go further than Rome though he might persuade her that Athens was not too far. We did not hear from him again.

I had the task of explaining to successful candidates the career they might expect if they opted for "hard" language training. It was understandable that our new entrants might not relish a further year or two of study immediately after seventeen years of education: their heart might not be in it; and most of them wanted to start work on solving the problems of the World. (They soon discovered that solutions did not come easily and that a problem might be solved only by creating a new one). We did, however, maintain a high standard of volunteer, and all those whom I sent on their way at this time reached Ambassadorial rank, one becoming the Permanent Under Secretary of the Office and Head of the Diplomatic Service.

I continued in my Acting B4 rank in Personnel Department until I was promoted substantively to that grade on, by chance, 23 October 1954, my 33rd birthday. This meant that in seniority I was way behind some younger colleagues who had come into the service through the post-war examinations and I would not get on very fast if "Buggins' Turn", the preference of the Civil Service Unions, applied. John Henniker-Major expressed surprise that I was only then receiving substantive B4 rank: "I thought you had been a B4 for years" he commented. I had, but on an acting basis, and was already on the maximum (£974.12s.0d per annum) of the B4 salary scale when "promoted". Another irony was that although I had been an acting B4 for so long I would be "on probation" in the grade for a further twelve months while I proved my ability to carry out the duties of the grade. Two years later I received my (first) Diplomatic Service Commission "constituting and appointing" me an Officer of Branch B of Her Majesty's Foreign Service with effect from 23 October 1954.

An interesting interlude in my time in Personnel Department was six weeks I spent as an additional assistant Private Secretary attending upon Anthony Eden, the Foreign Secretary. This interlude occurred after Eden had been to the United States for a serious operation. His doctors and advisers did not want him to return to active work in the Office but he wished to be kept informed. Eden was to live and work in the Foreign Secretary's official residence at No. 1 Carlton Gardens with me as his "minder", to use a word of later vogue but not then used. Evelyn Shuckburgh, the Principal Private Secretary, told me to keep Eden quiet and not to let him interfere. A tall order, I thought, and soon found it difficult to implement, especially when Selwyn Lloyd, the Acting Foreign Secretary, came to brief and consult Eden, who would thereafter itch to get back into the middle of the action. I discovered that Eden was a very vain man with the arrogance of his class: rules did not apply to him. I remember recommending to him that we should secure some confidential papers remaining on his desk at the end of the day, to be told that there was no danger of them being stolen, they should stay where they were and "we are not behind the Iron Curtain now". Later, in 1956, Eden was able to set aside the rules of Cabinet government in order to give himself room to pursue his vendetta against President Nasser of Egypt: this was the Suez crisis, of which more later.

While we were at home this time Christina and I set up home in a rented house in Hampton Hill from where commuting to Whitehall was easy. Our two children attended local schools, five year old Robin, having his first experience of school, made local friends and had the excitement of the schools' celebration of the Coronation of Queen Elizabeth the Second in 1953. We bought a television set to watch the Coronation, and to listen to the magnificent commentary thereon by Richard Dimbleby, and retained it for our entertainment and that of the children who were beguiled, particularly by Annette Mills and Muffin the Mule, Andy Pandy, and the Flower Pot Men. Children's Hour and Children's Favourites were still broadcast by the BBC. How simple and gentle children's entertainment was then compared with the complex, not to mention violent and weird fare, which the broadcasting companies dispense these days. The older theory appeared to be that children's entertainment should have a calming effect before early bed-time (6.00 p.m. for ours) whilst the current wisdom appears to be to disturb them. I suppose that they will survive as they have always done.

6

Middle East Centre for Arabic Studies (MECAS)

At the end of 1955 we travelled to Beirut to become students at the Middle East Centre for Arabic Studies in the village of Shemlan in the mountains above Beirut with a breathtaking view to the West across the Mediterranean. The sunsets were spectacular. We had still not travelled by air, the 1950s version of "post chaise and fast packet" being the Golden Arrow Pullman train from Victoria Station to Paris, and express train from Paris to Genoa (or Venice) and a passenger ship (the *Esperia* or *Enotria* of the Adriatica Line) from Italy to the Levant. These were beautifully found ships with high quality Italian crews for whom the passengers' needs never appeared to cause problems. The four days we spent on the cruise from Genoa to Beirut were idyllic and as good a holiday as could be found anywhere.

We were lucky too to have served in Genoa in 1950. One of the Consular clerks was a Mrs Rando, the Australian wife of the Commodore of the Italia merchant fleet. When she and the Commodore heard that we were travelling by the *Enotria* they persuaded the Captain and the Chief Engineer to give up their cabins on the bridge to the Lamb Family. This was very embarrassing since we were far from persuaded that it was necessary: the cabins allocated to us were adequate and comfortable; and such a dislocation of the personal arrangements of the ship's senior officers might not put us in good standing with them and their crew. But against four voluble Italians (Mrs Rando was as fluent as the other three) our protests went unheeded and we travelled to Beirut in style and on the best of terms with Captain and crew.

After arriving in Shemlan we stayed for a while in the local tourist hotel, Mulberry Lodge, before moving into one of four flats in a new block built for the purpose of accommodating students at the Centre. The landlord was a Shukri Hitti who, in the fashion of Yasser Arafat of the Palestine Liberation Organisation (PLO), always had a growth of beard suggesting that he had not shaved for three days. He and his wife were friendly and sympathetic landlords who valued what they considered to be a secure contract with the Centre. Shemlan was a Christian village although the so-called shaikh was a Druze. Everybody had a gun and at a village wedding the men continually fired feux de joie from the guns, which they had brought along to the celebration. Shukri Hitti told me on more than one occasion that there were guns stored in every house and that one day they would have to be used against the Muslims. A sad prophecy which has come true and destroyed a country.

The Centre was housed in a former silk factory that had once been fed by the activities of silkworms on local mulberry trees (hence the name of the local hotel). Its Director when we arrived was Mr Alan Trott, a distinguished Orientalist who had served as Ambassador to Saudi Arabia. He was a dedicated naturalist, given to keeping the bodies of birds he wished to study in the refrigerator in his kitchen. He was one of those men who is too brilliant at his own speciality to be able to pass it on successfully to others. He used to take my class for readings of the Koran when we had no real knowledge of Arabic or understanding of Islam. But Mr Trott derived much enjoyment for himself from his reading the Koran. James Craig was already the Chief Instructor at the Centre when I joined it and Alan Trott was soon succeeded by Donald Maitland, also a distinguished Foreign Office Arabist, but still on his way up to the highest echelons of the Diplomatic Service and eventually to the post of Permanent Under Secretary of the Department of Energy before his retirement as Sir Donald. Our studies prospered under the guidance of these distinguished Arabic scholars and I was pleased to pass out third in the order of merit in the final Foreign Service Higher Standard Arabic Examination (equivalent to Honours Degree standard) in March 1957, behind Patrick Wright, later the Permanent Under Secretary of the Foreign Office and Head of the Diplomatic Service, and Terry Clark, later Her Majesty's Ambassador to Iraq and Oman, both of whom were more than ten years my junior. My major problem in learning Arabic at the age of 35 was the absorption of vocabulary and pronunciation. I had less difficulty with the structure of the language but getting Arabic words to stay in my head was a problem. We used visiting cards, on one side of which we wrote the English word and on the other the Arabic and then carried these cards with us literally everywhere, turning them over and muttering the Arabic to ourselves. Reading the English-Arabic or Arabic-English dictionary was also a help. The fifteen months I was at MECAS was a hard but eventually worthwhile slog. Christina also studied Arabic, having said, when I told her of my Middle East ambitions, that if I was going to be an Arabist she too had better learn Arabic.

While we were at MECAS there took place an international confrontation which has been seen as the last gasp of British imperialism in the Middle East. This was the Suez crisis in 1956, brought about by the ambition of President Nasser to be master of his own land, Egypt, to rally the forces of Arab Nationalism throughout the Middle East under his banner and to seek military and financial help from the Soviet Bloc if he could not get it from the West. The American and British Governments overreacted and withdrew their offer to finance a development project close to Nasser's heart, a high dam on the Nile at Aswan. Nasser reacted by nationalising the privately-owned (by Western interests) Suez Canal. Eden saw this as a threat to the security of oil supplies from the Persian Gulf and the Suez Canal as vital to the security of Britain as it had once been for securing the sea passage to the Empire of India (independent as India and Pakistan since 1947).

Seeing Nasser as another Hitler, Eden, using Selwyn Lloyd, the Foreign Secretary, as his instrument, and without Cabinet authority, conspired with the French and Israeli Governments to attack Egypt and bring down Nasser and his Government. Superpower America did not, however, see matters in the same light. Alarmed by what they saw as a return to imperialism which would drive Nasser deeper into the embrace of the Russians, the United States forced Eden to accept a ceasefire, and the last attempt by a British Government to impose its will in the Middle East by force ended in humiliation.

The Suez adventure was seen as disastrous for British interests in the Middle East and, more narrowly, making the task of Foreign Office Arabists more demanding. Those en poste and in the Foreign Office were unanimously against the misguided adventure; and the corridor outside the Personnel Department was lined by members of the Service queuing up to resign. Fortunately most of them were persuaded to stand by to retrieve British fortunes in the Middle East. One Foreign Office student at MECAS did resign, but his value was not lost since he became a well-informed and distinguished journalist specialising in Arab affairs. The British debacle at Suez did not discourage the rest of us; and neither did an Arab terrorist bomb attack against the Centre. Terry Clark was slightly injured but little damage was done to the fabric of the Centre or to its ability to teach. In the Middle East the Centre had acquired a false reputation as a "school for spies" and for British Imperialists at that. It was also a soft target for the perpetrators of the terrorist attack since at night the only occupants of the unguarded, security–free Centre were the unmarried students who lived in. The Army officers who were studying Arabic at the Centre, at the time of the Suez, were recalled to their units but none of them saw any action; their time would have been better employed at their books in Shemlan.

Shemlan provided a further adventure in schooling for Elizabeth and Robin since they had to travel down the mountain by taxi to Beirut in the care of the taxi driver, another member of the Hitti family, to attend respectively a Christian Girls School run on an English curriculum and the British Community School, both of which were admirable. Christina and I never discovered how much Arabic our two children picked up from the villagers of Shemlan but we suspected that they understood more than we did even if they were reluctant to speak it. In 1970 Robin attended a six-month course at the Centre as part of his studies of Arabic at Brasenose College at Oxford and went on to follow my footsteps into the Diplomatic Service.

Lebanon was a beautiful country, but the Lebanese had some unattractive traits. It seemed to me that whatever subject might start a conversation with them, in three minutes flat they were into their favourite subject: money. (In this they foreshadowed the British Conservative Government from 1979). They were also ready to fawn upon the rich visitors from the oil-producing countries; but I remember a garage-owner in Souk alGharb, the nearest large village to Shemlan, shouting "Animal!" to a departing Gulf Shaikh after the latter had paid well for the crawliest Uriah Heep attentions - and when the Shaikh in his American car was well out of earshot. They were also largely unhelpful to foreign students of Arabic, laughing at the mistakes and not slowing their natural voluble flow for the benefit of the foreigner. I suspected that the Lebanese were snobbish about Arabic because they were not really Arabs but one of the Mediterranean peoples who live around that Sea. The Egyptians are not really Arabs either but the product of an ancient civilisation living on a river, the Nile, and the Mediterranean Sea; but their deep culture enables them to use their Arabic sensibly with foreigners. They also have a sense of humour, which I did not find in the Lebanese (except at my expense and my Arabic). As an example I remember an Egyptian guide touting for business on the quayside at Alexandria calling up to me in early 1957 in the aftermath of the Suez debacle, "Don't be afraid about coming ashore: we are all Irish here!" The Egyptians, alone among the people of the Middle East, also have the ability to laugh at themselves and to make political jokes about their leaders. In the time of President Gamal Abdul Nasser there were, it was said, three candidates for a job in Egypt. Each candidate was asked to give the sum of two plus two. The first candidate, an Englishman, said "Four, Sir", the second, a Jew, enquired if he was buying or selling and the third, an Egyptian, replied "Four, plus baksheesh." Who got the job? An Army officer.

At the end of my course at Shemlan I was posted back to London to brief myself for going to the Embassy in Jedda, the Foreign Secretary Selwyn Lloyd having thought that, at a meeting at the United Nations in New York with the Saudi Arabian Crown Prince Faisal (later King Faisal), agreement had been reached to resume diplomatic relations between Britain and the Saudi Kingdom which had been broken off at the time of the Suez crisis. It eventually appeared that Prince Faisal remembered a different version of the conversation and had no intention of welcoming British diplomats back to Jedda. I was thus at a loose end and available for posting to the Political Residency in

Bahrain; but before that happened a substantial development in my career took place.

7

Promotion, Bahrain and Trade Promotion

On 3 July 1957 John Henniker-Major kindly wrote to me:

I am very pleased that you passed the Higher Standard Arabic examination so well. This is a real feather in your cap.

On 12 July 1957 Personnel Department told me that "the question of your possible transfer to Branch A is under consideration. Could you come up for a small Board on Wednesday July 17 at 11.30 a.m.? It will meet in the Chief Clerk's room under his chairmanship."

The Chief Clerk of the Foreign Office is the Deputy Under Secretary in charge of Administration, the title deriving from the time when all members of the Foreign Officer under the politically-appointed Ministers were Clerks of whom, obviously, the Chief Clerk was in charge. (In 1790 when the Foreign Office first took shape and a Permanent Under Secretary was appointed with a salary of £1500 a year, this official was assisted by a Chief Clerk, two Senior Clerks, nine Junior Clerks, a Latin Secretary and a "Decipherer of Letters"). At the time of my "small Board" the Chief Clerk was Sir Roderick Barclay, a member of the banking family who had a distinguished career ending as H.M. Ambassador to Belgium. On the way he was Principal Private Secretary to Ernest Bevin from 1949 to 1951 and has recorded his experiences with that great man in his book *Ernest Bevin and the Foreign Office* published in 1975. (When I was Ambassador to Norway in the 1970s his son-in-law, Andrew Palmer, who married Sir Roderick's daughter, Davina, was my Political Counsellor and Head of Chancery). The other members of the Board were Sir Thomas Bromley, who entered the Consular Service in 1935 and retired as Ambassador to Ethiopia, and John Henniker-Major, whom I have already mentioned. I remember chatting pleasantly with the Board, from whom I gathered that the Foreign Office had awaited the outcome of my efforts at MECAS before considering further my transfer to the Senior Branch of the Diplomatic Service. I must have persuaded the Board that I was worth a place in Branch A since on 22 August 1957 I received the following letter:

> Sir,
>
> *I have to inform you that you have been promoted, subject to the successful completion of a probationary period of two years, to be an officer of the Seventh Grade in Branch A of Her Majesty's Foreign Service with effect from the 17th August 1957. Your seniority in the Grade will take effect from the 1st of July 1957.*
>
> *I am, Sir,*
> *Your obedient Servant*
>
> *(For the Secretary of State)*

I was now a First Secretary and the first Clerical Officer to be promoted into the diplomatic ranks proper of the Foreign Service. I was now a diplomat, or a diplomatist as the more purist students of the theory and practice of diplomacy would have it. Thus Sir Harold Nicolson, who from the 1930s established himself as Britain's leading writer on diplomacy, and whose book *Diplomacy*, first published in 1939, has remained required reading for aspiring diplomats, had no doubt that the ideal diplomatist has seven specific diplomatic virtues: Truthfulness, Precision, Calm, Good Temper, Patience, Modesty and Loyalty. (Nicolson said that he took for granted Intelligence, Knowledge, Discernment, Prudence, Hospitality, Charm, Industry, Courage and Tact). Fortunately for my ego, which was adequately satisfied by my promotion, Personnel Department never told me whether or not I met Harold Nicolson's ideal.

In my negotiations with the Roumanian authorities on administrative and consular affairs I had taken a step towards practising diplomacy, defined by Harold Nicolson as "the management of international relations by negotiation; the method by which these relations are adjusted and managed by ambassadors and envoys; the business or art of the diplomatist." Adam Watson, a former member of the Diplomatic Service, sub-titled his book *Diplomacy* (1982) "The Dialogue between States", but admitted that "A complex activity of this kind is difficult to comprehend in a single phrase". He later usefully explains 'the distinction between "foreign policy" as the substance of a state's relations with other powers and agencies and the purposes it hopes to achieve by these relations, and "diplomacy" as the process of dialogue and negotiation by which states in a system conduct their relations and pursue their purposes by means short of war.'

To borrow from Shakespeare, on such a full sea was I now afloat, and I must take the current as it served or lose my venture, since once more was I on probation, for two years. In addition to Nicolson's dicta there were other wise and noble sayings to guide me. Nicolson had introduced us to the epigram of the Marquis de Talleyrand "Et surtout pas trop de zèle" which Nicolson translated as "And above everything do not allow yourself to become excited about your work." This was not good advice, a misapplication of "the stiff upper lip" which probably explains the French joke: "When I first saw him I thought that he was very, very ill; but then I learned that he was a British diplomat." It is surely only human to feel excitement when engaged in some pursuit, the outcome of which might bring pleasure to one and all. The modern expression "the adrenalin is flowing" reflects this. What I had already learned about the way of the world, both as a fighter-bomber pilot and as a public servant, was that I must not become emotionally involved with the tasks entrusted to me, yet have the enthusiasm to tackle them successfully. In my youth at St Paul's Church in Sketty, I had been impressed by St Paul's injunction to the Romans in Chapter 12 of his Epistle "Be not wise in your own conceits. Recompense to no man evil for evil. Provide things honest in the sight of all men. If it be possible, as much as liveth in you, live peaceably with all men." And then in the Royal Air Force I had learned Murphy's Law (known as Sod's Law to the airmen) that if something can go wrong, it will. So keep your wits about you and be ready for the unexpected. Also, like all my generation, I had listened to the monologues of Sir George Robey, the music hall entertainer, who in one of his perorations enjoined young men to "temper your enthusiasm with a modicum of reserve", a much more correct translation of Talleyrand's epigram than that of Nicolson.

With all this good advice and eighteen years of experience in Foreign Office, Royal Air Force and Foreign Service behind me, where would I go to practice the profession of Diplomacy? The prospect of Jedda having fallen away, the Office responded to a plea for help from the Political Resident in the Persian Gulf and posted me to the Residency in Bahrain, as a supernumerary First Secretary for such duties as the Political Resident should decide.

During the Nineteenth Century, in defence of India, the Jewel in the Crown, Britain established its influence over the Arab Shaikhdoms of the Persian Gulf (Kuwait, Bahrain, Qatar and the seven Trucial States) and the Sultanate of Muscat and Oman. The British Resident at Bushire, who reported to the Government of India, became virtually the ruler of the Gulf. In 1948, after the Independence of India and Pakistan, the Political Resident moved his seat to Bahrain and reported to the Foreign Office in London.

In 1957 the Sultan of Muscat and Oman asked for British help against a rebellion by the Iman of Oman who was seeking, amongst other things, the independence of Oman, which he claimed had been assured by the Treaty of Sib of 1920. In this he was supported by a powerful tribal leader, Sulaiman bin Himyar, "the Lord of the Green Mountain", who was finally brought down by the SAS and RAF in 1959. So in 1957 the Political Resident, Sir Bernard Burrows, had a war on his hands and, as he said in a letter welcoming my appointment to his staff, "we are fairly hard pressed and can well do with some more help."

I had seen the oil industry in action in Roumania, the authorities there not seeming to worry about trips through the Ploesti oilfields on my way to Sinaia; and the Chancery files on the expropriation of British oil interests there had occasionally come my way. But now in Bahrain, in the duties I took on, I got a much closer look at the way of the oil world and began my own very real interest in the international oil industry and particularly the geopolitics that surrounded it. I also became responsible for the Residency end of the Trucial States Development Programme through which HMG were financing development in those seven sheikhdoms, at that time without oil and seemingly without any prospect of having any. The actual administrator of the programme was the Political Agent in Dubai, the Political Resident's man in the Trucial States with the far from easy task of managing relations with and among the seven Rulers of those States.

I was a "spare wheel on the coach" for only four months, becoming the Commercial Secretary of the Residency at the beginning of 1958. I kept the oil portfolio, having decided that this was far too interesting to lose. Commercial work, or trade promotion, had recently become fashionable. Pre-war diplomats would have been horrified if they had been asked to do such work; the Commercial Attaché at an Embassy would not have expected to have seen much of His Excellency the Ambassador: rather like my experience with Sir Noel Charles in Rome. The formation of the Commercial Diplomatic Service in 1919 did not improve the lot of trade promoters. According to Geoffrey Moorhouse, in his book (1977) *The Diplomats*, Commercial Attachés were not asked to dine at the embassy.

The Commercial Secretary was very much a part of the team in the Political Residency. In addition to his principal task of helping British exporters with market and tariff information, reports and advice on sales opportunities and suitable local agents, his visits to the Arab merchants in the suqs (bazaars) of Bahrain, Qatar, the Trucial States and Muscat provided opportunities of discovering local views on matters beyond trade which provided useful information for the Residency. I did not cover Kuwait since this had already produced an oil-wealth-based market sufficiently large to justify the Political Agent in that city-state having his own Commercial Department. There was also a Financial Counsellor, from HM Treasury, in Kuwait originally appointed to close the "Kuwait Gap" through which non-convertible sterling became convertible with consequential profits for the Kuwaiti dealers and losses to the British economy. Kuwait and the rest of the Gulf were at that time part of the Sterling Area and one of my tasks in Bahrain, under the guidance of the Treasury Counsellor, was that of Exchange Controller. Most applications for convertible sterling for trading purposes were self-evidently bona fide, but the occasional one would raise doubts, and the question whether a quick turn through the Beirut money market (two hours behind the Gulf) was a prime objective. But no cases serious enough to warrant action arose during my time as Exchange Controller. Twenty years later, when I was Ambassador to Kuwait, sterling was again a matter of active concern for me when HMG, through the Governor of the Bank of England, Gordon (later Lord) Richardson and the Deputy Governor, Kit (later Sir Kit) McMahon, negotiated with the Kuwait Government the run-down of its sterling balances in London which had become too great a liability for the less prosperous Britain of the 1970s. Later, of course, after the Conservative Government of Mrs Thatcher declared sterling fully convertible in 1979, one wondered what the fuss had been all about and then remembered that problems can only be dealt with within the context of the received wisdom of the day. "Dealt with", not necessarily solved; moved along to contribute to another problem later: for example, the Kuwait Government's unwelcome purchase of BP shares in 1988.

My own attitude to diplomatic participation in trade promotion was positive from the beginning since it was clear that British businessmen needed a lot of help if their parent companies were to manufacture and sell the goods that the Arab market of the Gulf required. Writing now after many years' experience of trade promotion, I hold the view that business firms, business organisations and businessmen are not always organised, alert and suitable for their jobs; and that no official export promotion machinery can fill these gaps in industry. I recall that in 1959 I toured British industry speaking on the profitable business opportunities available in the Gulf. I remember two outstanding occasions when "experienced" businessmen put me in my place. I went to the Rover factory and explained the ever-increasing market for Landrovers opening generally but particularly in the Trucial States. I was told that the Rover Company was content with the level of its Landrover production and would not produce more. Rover lost the market to the Japanese Toyota Landcruiser. I went to Leicester to talk to some people in the wool trade and explained to them the demand for fine woollen cloth for the bisht (the Arab cloak) and other apparel in the Gulf. "Now, lad," said he-who-knew-all, "I've been in this business for forty years and I've never sold wool to Gulf." He refused to admit that it was time he started. The motor industry let us down again by refusing to install air-conditioning and cassette players as standard fittings in British cars for the Gulf, preferring to offer them as "optional extras": "the Arabs can have them if they ask for them". Again the Japanese provided what the market demanded. There were, fortunately, others who did heed one's advice; for example, a consulting engineer who I insisted should visit Dubai even though he had no intention of going there when he called on me in Bahrain. He went and his firm continued to enjoy the trust of the local authorities and profitable business for years thereafter.

The extent to which the British Government should help British trade and industry to sell their goods and services abroad has been a matter for discussion since the reign of Elizabeth I, when the industrial, commercial and social system of our country was brought under national, instead of municipal, control. It was in the 16th Century that Britain established its first Consulate, at Aleppo, specifically to help British trade with the Levant, Central Asia and the Orient. These were also the days of the establishment of the great trading companies which, following the discovery by English and European sailors that the seas were not barriers but channels of communication, led to the establishment of Empire. This also played its part in developing the responsibility of government for the regulation of trade. A good and bad example is Imperial Preference which, while Britain had an Empire, ensured captive markets for British goods and services; but after Britain lost its Empire, British trade and industry could not change the mentality with which Imperial Preference had imbued it and failed to grasp that goods and services have to be marketed as well as sold.

The question is: how does one measure the effectiveness of Government intervention, how does one organise this and how does one organise and measure the work performed by the Diplomatic Service around the world in carrying out its commercial duties? There have always been complaints. For example, a *Times* leading article of 7 May 1832:

> *Perhaps Lord Palmerston, if the subject is not too coarse or too trivial to occupy the polite attention of so fine a gentleman, will order some inquiry to be made respecting certain irregularities in the transmission of mercantile correspondence from Lisbon. A hint may be necessary, if not in the case of the Lisbon ambassador, yet to some others of our noble functionaries, whose minds being dedicated to sublimer affairs, have forgot or never learned that Great Britain is actually a commercial kingdom and does really derive some of its wealth and importance from trade and manufactures.*

Plus ça change plus c'est la même chose. Nearly 150 years later, on 2 August 1978, HMG issued a White Paper stating that the promotion of the prosperity of the United Kingdom is one of Britain's overseas objectives, on a par with safeguarding the security of our country; and that economic matters are inextricably part of British foreign policy and that Britain's need and interests as a trading nation will inevitably continue to be a decisive influence on the country's foreign policy. Earlier, in 1964, a Report of the Committee on Representational Services Overseas (the Plowden Committee) (Cmnd.2276) had recommended that economic and commercial work should be regarded as a first charge on the resources of the Diplomatic Service. The perils of taking this injunction too literally have been well brought out in Sir Anthony Parsons' book *The Pride and the Fall* (1984) about his Mission to Iran from 1974 to 1979. Sir Anthony tells us that his "Embassy was primarily organised as an agency for the promotion of British exports and for the general commercial, financial and economic interests of Britain. This was true both of the civilian and military staff, while even the political officers had a brief to be on the lookout for fresh export opportunities. Even the British Council was organised to concentrate on commercial aspects. Study of the internal political situation in Iran was a subsidiary activity." Sir Anthony's book is, in a way, a lament for the downgrading of political intelligence as the priority requirement for the overall promotion of British interests, in whatever foreign field they may lie. The essential truth to be grasped by all practitioners and students of diplomacy is that relations between and among independent sovereign states are political and can never be evaluated solely on commercial, economic, financial, cultural or military considerations.

The 1978 White Paper entered an important caveat: export promotion could not be a pre-eminent requirement of overseas representation in all countries of the world... an assessment of the British interest could not therefore be confined either generally, or in any one country, to economic or export considerations alone. This caveat reflected my own belief, from the time I started in commercial work in 1957, that such work does not exist in a separate compartment detached from the rest of the work of an Embassy or Consulate. This has been frequently misunderstood in Britain, even producing, during my own career, the contradiction of an instruction that "Ambassadors will concern themselves more with commercial work; the Commercial Department of an Embassy will not be located in the Embassy but downtown in the business centre." Shades of the separateness quoted by Geoffrey Moorhouse and referred to above. If commercial work is to have the eminence that HMG wish it to have, it must be treated as an integral part of the Embassy effort and its practitioners work in close physical and mental liaison with their colleagues in the other departments of the Mission. All are acquiring information and contacts, which have to be sifted and exchanged to ensure that the Mission is obtaining from them the maximum benefit in all fields. Cross-pollination, rather than the Commercial Department getting all the pollen. When I acquired a Mission of my own I coined the term "total diplomacy" for the effort that I wished my staff and myself to make. I found little difference between the fundamentals of briefing a RAF squadron for a raid and briefing the political, economic, commercial, military, information and consular departments of my Embassy for an operation to win foreign hearts and minds in the British interest, whichever of the departments might have prime responsibility therefore. I was very pleased to read in the 1978 White Paper that the closest analogy to the function of a Head of Mission is that of a Captain of a ship; it could have made the comparison with a Squadron Leader but very few ex-RAF pilots have been counted among our political governors, who tend more to Army and Navy backgrounds.

In managing my Commercial Department in Bahrain I soon came to realise that we could not respond with equal time and effort to all requests for help from British trade and industry. There was no limit to the work which in theory we could undertake; but resources were limited (a Second Secretary and a locally-engaged Market Officer in addition to myself, and a share of the Residency's secretarial services) making selectivity essential. Provided that we did not give needless offence to importunate businessmen we could count on support in London for the intelligence exercise of selectivity if this should give rise to complaint. As it did from time to time, in Bahrain and later in my career at Kuwait and Oslo, with dire threats to report me to the Prime Minister or any other of our Governors with whom the complainant claimed to be on the closest of terms. But we also required defence from London since the Board (later Department) of Trade in trying to be all things to all men – there are votes in giving the voter what he wants, or thinks he wants – would sometimes set priorities which were unrealistic. I remember that in Kuwait in the late 1970s, one priority commodity for trade promotion was greetings stationery in English. Since at the time there was a construction boom in progress and we were engaged in selling 165 Chieftain tanks to the Kuwait Army, I gave greetings stationery a low profile. Later, in Norway, it seemed to me that an effort to influence the Norwegian oil industry towards a British share in their multi-million dollar offshore projects should outweigh any effort on behalf of consumer goods, of which the Norwegians manufactured their own to their taste. (They make very good toothbrushes). We had already lost the motor car market in Norway which, pre-war, had been supplied almost entirely by the Morris and Austin companies.

It was my good fortune in Bahrain to have the economic and financial work on my desk and to have the whole of the southern Gulf as my territory. An officer in a commercial department of an Embassy is at his most useful in commercial work when he has thoroughly grasped the economic background to the market; and since Bahrain had for long been an entrepôt for the Gulf (and eastern Arabia) it was important to have a detailed understanding of how the increasing prosperity of the other Gulf and Arabian States was influencing the way in which they all handled their trade. All wanted to have their own import agencies and not to be dependent on Bahrain or elsewhere for ordering the goods and services they wanted. This nationalist (and profit-improving) ambition created problems for the established agents located in Bahrain and Kuwait and for their principals in the United Kingdom, who were in danger of offending someone somewhere in the Gulf and losing the influence in the market that had been carefully developed over the years. The advice I gave to British business had to be that the advantage lay in an agent in every territory, either directly appointed by the principal or through an arrangement between the existing main agent and a partner in each territory. This was easier to say than to do and much patient work was put in by British principals in keeping old and new friends in the Gulf happy with the new arrangements they wished to introduce for the promotion and distribution of their products. The Bahraini merchants did not like the advice I gave. They thought that since I was stationed in Bahrain I should support them against all claimants to a share in their Gulf-wide trade. Over the years as the oil-producing states of the Gulf became ever more wealthy there was plenty of trade for all to make more, far more, than an adequate living from agencies or sub-agencies.

I mentioned above my good fortune in combining economic and commercial work in a wide and expanding market. Businessmen, whose livelihood depends on profit, are easily and justifiably disappointed by a shortfall in the knowledge that they might reasonably expect a diplomat to have about the place where he is stationed. If disappointed they will probably think of him as did Wilkie Collins, the 19th Century novelist: "A professional diplomat is an empty man, carefully trained to look full on public occasions". Nobody could apply this description to the modern British diplomat. No longer can the Ambassador sit in his study and let the world and the work come to him. The international framework within which British foreign policy operates has changed out of all recognition since 1945. No longer Mistress of an Empire and of the Seas which bound that Empire together and provided the routes for profitable trade on British terms, Britain is now a member of a European Union and, with its partners therein, increasingly required to act in concert in matters touching on the Community's relations with the rest of the World and increasingly involved in competition in international markets with them and the other industrialised countries, Old and New. Since foreign policy is about what has to be done and diplomacy about how to do it, clearly the British diplomat has had to respond to the changing conditions of his country's national existence.

A changing condition to which Christina and I had to adjust was separation from our two children. There was no school suitable and open to them in Bahrain in the 1950s and both had to be left in boarding schools in Britain, Elizabeth at Monmouth School for Girls and Robin at St Neots Preparatory School at Eversley in Hampshire. I am sure that if we had had the whole of our career in the United Kingdom, Christina and I would not have sent the children to boarding school; only "the exigencies of the Service" forced us to do so. Our second daughter, Kathryn, was born in Bahrain in 1959, the first "Residency baby" to be born in the new maternity hospital. When Christina replied "A girl" to the enquiry from an Arab ward orderly about the sex of the baby, the orderly commented "Ah! Never mind!" reflecting the Arab belief that it is more blessed to bear a son than a daughter.

The two Political Residents under whom I worked in Bahrain were not cast in the same mould. The first, Sir Bernard Burrows, was tall, quite heavily moustached and somewhat silent. Christina remembers an occasion at his dinner table when he listened patiently and silently to a lengthy exposition by the lady guest of honour of a book she had read. Sir Bernard spoke "I think you misunderstood that book". He was, however, kinder than this remark, taken by itself, would suggest and I was grateful for the guidance he gave me in my first post as a "diplomat" in Branch A of the Diplomatic Service.

Sir George Middleton succeeded Sir Bernard. He had started his career in the Consular Service and had much experience of trade promotion, telling me that in his formative years he had been Vice-Consul in New York with responsibility for watching over the "garment district". He was interested in my commercial work far more than his predecessor and took part in it himself. A kind letter of thanks I received from a British merchant house when I left Bahrain referred to the gap that would be left by the departure of Sir George and myself.

Before I left Bahrain my appointment to branch A was confirmed, I received my Commission as an Officer of that Branch and, as John Henniker-Major put it in one of his characteristically kind letters, "there are no longer any conditions attached to your incorporation in Branch A, of which you are now a fully-fledged member".

Bahrain has remained in my mind the most pleasant of the Gulf States. Never very rich, never very poor, not over-blessed with oil wealth, Bahrain has supported itself by trade and, until the 1950s, by pearling, the Japanese cultured pearl bringing to an end the diving for the natural pearls of the Gulf. Bahrain has always been sensibly governed, the Ruler in 1925, Shaikh Hamad bin Isa AlKlalifah, employing a British Adviser, Sir Charles Belgrave, to help him put the government of his shaikhdom on a modern footing. Sir Charles's reminiscences in his book *Personal Column* (1960) are worth reading. Shaikh Hamad's wise government was carried on by his successors, providing a tolerant Sunni state in which foreigners were welcome and ostentation eschewed. (I was disappointed to read in *The Times* in February 1989 that the then Ruler, Shaikh Isa, wished to knock his London residence [a listed building] around to provide himself with a Throne Room. This does not sound like Bahraini commonsense).

The good start, which Shaikh Hamad and Charles Belgrave, not to mention exceptional Bahrainis such as Yusuf Shirawi, later the Minister for Oil and Development, gave to 20th Century Bahrain, was not emulated elsewhere in the Gulf. All the others had that raw taste of administrations hastily cobbled together to respond to and to spend the oil wealth, which eventually came the way of all of them. But money talks loud in the Gulf and Arabia; and the other States of the area, all of them wealthier by far than Bahrain, now have the loudest voices.

I have mentioned the importance attached to trade promotion as a function of British diplomacy. Following the advent of the Conservative Government under Mrs Thatcher in 1979, with its policy and her passion for privatisation and hiving off, I had been expecting a radical proposal that trade promotion should be returned to the private sector. It is possible to visualise an "Overseas Representation Company" funded by British trade and industry and providing advisory, information and representational services for companies willing to pay for them. The saving in manpower and money in the Diplomatic Service would be considerable; and there are many who still say that the burden of trade promotion should be lifted from the Service: that in accepting commercial work as "a first charge upon the resources of the Service" the Foreign Office surrendered to pressure, to fashion, at the expense of the political work which it alone can do in the international context. The Government "Think Tank" Report of 1977 said that the Foreign Office and the Diplomatic Service "operates at an unacceptable standard of excellence", an absurd criticism of the high standards set by and for them. Those high standards have been increasingly required, as political implications and diplomatic consequences multiply, following the increasing trend towards the economic and financial unitisation of the World: 'globalisation'. There are powerful arguments for releasing the essential resources of the Foreign Office and Diplomatic Service for an enhanced politico-economic rôle by entrusting trade promotion to those who benefit directly from it.

8

Foreign Office: The Oil Desk

I returned to the Foreign Office in May 1961 for a few months in the Arabian Department watching over British relations with the Sultanate of Muscat and Oman. This was an interesting and amusing time for one particular reason: I got to know the Sultan, Said bin Taimur Al bu Said. Born in 1910 and educated in a British school in India, Sultan Said succeeded his father, Taimur, in 1932, when the latter retired to Bombay, fed up with the problems of ruling. Said inherited a bankrupt state and was forced into an attention to detail which became obsessive. I had visited Muscat from Bahrain and had been told of the absolute power of the Sultan, the sole arbiter of everything which touched his Sultanate. One thing which was "out" was progress and development and the current joke was that the Sultanate and its Ruler would have to be dragged kicking and screaming out of the 14th Century. In 1958 HMG had negotiated an agreement with the Sultan under which Britain would provide him with military and economic development assistance. The money for the latter was to be paid to the Sultan for him to disburse as he saw fit; no conditions were attached by HMG. The British-educated Sultan stood on the letter of the agreement and resisted all pressure brought upon him by British Ministers, the Political Resident in the Gulf and the British Consul-General in Muscat to speed the pace of development. An absorbing account of these events is found in Ian Skeet's *"Oman Before 1970"* (1974).

Thus, when the Sultan visited Britain in 1961, the Government were ready to do battle with him and I was sent off to be in attendance upon him and to report his mood. I found him established in a suite in the Dorchester Hotel, a reasonable and intelligent man to all appearances who enjoyed general conversation over lunch and over tea, which he took regularly at 4.00 p.m. every afternoon and always included chocolate cake, which he cut himself. But he made it clear to me that there would be no discussion of Anglo-Sultanate affairs over our meals together; such discussion would take place at the right time in the right place, which were not the restaurants of the Dorchester Hotel. HMG got nowhere with him and he ruled in his own way until 1970, when he was deposed and succeeded by his son Qabus. He died soon afterwards, before he could see what his son had done to bring the Sultanate into the 20th Century with the oil wealth which poured into the Sultanate from 1967.

1961 was also the year that Britain responded to an appeal for military assistance from Kuwait, threatened with invasion by Iraq, which had a long-standing claim, as a successor state to the Ottoman Empire, to Kuwaiti territory. Fortunately HMS Bulwark, a commando carrier, was in the Gulf and was able to land forces immediately in Kuwait. The troops were there, on and beyond the Matla Ridge, an escarpment to the north of Kuwait City, throughout the Summer, when the temperature in the shade can reach 55 degrees Centigrade, refreshed by local sellers of ice-cream and Coca-Cola, until the British Force was replaced by an army from Arab States friendly to Kuwait. Iraq did not attempt an invasion.

British troops, wherever they have gone in the world, have been quick to sum up succinctly the local scene. During my time in the RAF I had heard versions of *The Shaiba Blues* and *The Basra War*, composed by RAF airmen stationed in Iraq. I cannot now remember the former but the latter described what the local population would do to aircrew unlucky enough to come down in the desert:

> *In the year Anno Domini One Nine Two Four*
> *In the Kingdom of Basra there started a war*
> *And if you go flying you'd better watch out*
> *If your engine conks out you'll have no hope at all.*

I have substituted "hope" for a word describing a part of the male anatomy. The British soldier rose to the challenge of Kuwait:

> *O land of cloudless, burning skies,*

Of sand and dust storms, sweat and flies,
Of women shrouded to the eyes – Kuwait.

The summer temperature's sky high,
The liquor ration may run dry,
Mother! What a place to die – Kuwait.

Down in Hades, Satan stirred.
Cor! Strike me scarlet! He averred,
I've learnt another dirty word – Kuwait.

O Kasim, hurry up and come,
With bugle, trumpet, fife and drum,
You don't know what you're getting, chum - Kuwait.

The reference to "Kasim" in the last of the soldier's verses is to the then dictator of Iraq.

Kuwait has always been independent and had not been constrained by the British protection, which they had enjoyed since 1899, and which they called for in enhanced military form in 1961. When I visited Kuwait in 1982 at the time of Britain's successful military action in the Falklands, I found that many Kuwaitis of some seniority professed to believe that although Kuwait had renounced British protection in 1961, there was a secret treaty which guaranteed British military assistance if Kuwait's independence was threatened. "If you would do it for the Falklands, surely you would do it for us" was the theme. And, of course, Britain was there to expel the Iraqis from Kuwait after Saddam Hussein's invasion of 1990.

In 1962 I moved within the Foreign Office to become Assistant Head of the Economic Relations Department, with which task went "the Oil Desk". I was the fourth occupant of this desk, which had been established in 1951 at the time of the "Mossadeq Crisis" in Iran when the Foreign Office were forced to recognise that British oil interests could not be left entirely in the hands of British Petroleum and Shell and that there was a foreign policy dimension which required day-to-day attention. Peter Ramsbotham (later Sir Peter, and HM Ambassador in Washington) was the first occupant of the desk, to be followed by Robert Belgrave, who left the Office for a distinguished career with British Petroleum, Peter Male, who retired as HM Ambassador to Czechoslovakia, and me.

The pace of the international oil world had quickened after the Second World War. Saudi Arabia, Kuwait and Iran began exporting in increasing quantities; Britain and Europe became dependent on oil supplies from the Gulf area, the United States having moved from being a major exporter of oil to being a nett importer. The leverage on the international oil companies of the governments of the oil-producing countries also increased. In 1950, the Arabian American Oil Company (ARAMCO) agreed to renegotiate their agreement with the Saudi Government, moving to a 50-50 division of profits, a substantial concession. In Iran, the Anglo-Iranian Oil Company (AIOC), wholly-owned by British Petroleum, had been negotiating for some time a supplemental agreement with the Iranian Government which would, however, fall far short of the terms ARAMCO were willing to offer Saudi Arabia. HMG trusted BP to bring about an agreement between AIOC and Iran, which would have regard to the political and economic essentials of the post-war oil world. This trust was misplaced, the Company's lack of political awareness stemming from the Chairman, Sir William Fraser, described by Kenneth Younger, the Minister of State in the Foreign Office in a memorandum of October 1951, as having "the contempt of a Glasgow accountant for anything which cannot be shown on a balance sheet" (an attitude which, to my frustration, I found prevailed into the 1980s in an oil company with which I was associated after my retirement from the Diplomatic Service. But I forced myself to remember that British oil companies are not political instruments of the British Government and have no obligation to consult the national interest: as Prime Minister Heath discovered during the 1973 oil crisis when he learned that the oil companies would treat the United Kingdom as just another customer when sharing out available oil supplies). BP's refusal to follow the ARAMCO example brought the Iranian Government under Prime Minister Mossadeq to nationalise AIOC. The settlement, which followed the downfall of Mossadeq, established a new Anglo-American consortium to exploit Iran's oil in which BP would have only a 40% share, with American companies taking 46% and Royal Dutch Shell (which is only 40% British owned) taking 14%. The United States Government had a much clearer and more certain view of the direction they wished Middle East oil to take: as much of it as possible under American control. (An absorbing American account of these days is given in Ambassador George McGhee's book *Envoy to the Middle World* [1983]).

The American oil companies were as politically obtuse as the British, Dutch and French in 1960 when the international companies unilaterally reduced the price of Middle East crude oil in disregard of a 1958 Declaration by the Arab Governments meeting in Cairo that that price should not be reduced without consultation with them. Later in 1960 the Organisation of Petroleum producing Countries (OPEC) was founded. The first "OPEC Crisis" soon followed when OPEC, under its Iranian Secretary-General, Rouhani, pressed the companies for further agreements on the pricing of oil, including a modest increase of one United States cent per barrel (about a 0.5% increase). It was in this situation, once again "the end of civilisation as we know it", according to the international oil companies, that I took over the oil desk.

The Foreign Office held regular meetings with BP and Shell to discuss the international oil situation but bent over backwards not to give advice, only to provide political information, since HMG still saw the companies as an essential, independent buffer between the governments of the oil-producing countries and the governments of the consuming countries. In this HMG were under the misapprehension that the companies would have regard to the national interest, whereas the Companies Act laid upon them as a first duty the interests of their shareholders; and, although HMG was at that time a majority shareholder in BP, the Companies Act did not envisage respect for a shareholder's political interests. When in 1988 the Kuwait Government appeared to be on the way to a significant shareholding in BP, the latter was quick to plead the national interest and cause HMG to intervene politically with the Kuwait Government to secure a reduction in their holding in BP. This action contradicted the Conservative Government's attachment to the principles of the free market and encouragement of unrestricted inward investment into Britain. The action confirmed that "oil is different" and, as by far the major commodity in international trade, requires a separate set of political rules to control its impact on the economy and governance of a country. The Kuwait Government miscalculated, making in 1988 a mistake opposite to that made by HMG thirty years earlier. The Kuwait Government failed to understand that no State oil company, such as the Kuwait Petroleum Corporation, and no State financial institution, such as the Kuwait Investment Office in London, which was buying the BP shares, can be other than a political instrument of the parent government and must act in that government's national interests.

BP and Shell were generous and unstinting in the briefings and information they gave me and my education in the oil industry proceeded apace. While admiring both for their mastery of international oil operations and the skill with which they promoted their interests with HMG, I detected a substantial difference between the approaches of the two companies. BP, wholly British, was very much a City of London shareholding company with all the caution which that suggests; Shell, the British side of Royal Dutch Shell, of which the Netherlands owned 60%, was truly an international company with a wider outlook. BP was suspicious of the Foreign Office; in being abrasively sarcastic about the Foreign Office and all its doings, one of their people gave away more about a certain attitude in BP than he intended. Shell treated the Department as a useful player in the World's Game whose views were worth listening to (and no doubt checking against those of the Netherlands Foreign Ministry and against their own world-wide intelligence). Both knew well that HMG would not interfere with their management of their commercial interests but BP were more wary because of HMG's holding, at that time, of 51% of BP's shares.

On one occasion I visited Washington DC, accompanying an Under-Secretary from the Ministry of Fuel and Power (later Energy) for an exchange of views with the State Department on the Middle East Oil situation. The Under-Secretary spoke with an Anglo-Scottish accent, which our American counterparts found difficult to comprehend. He was also given to the use of British colloquialisms, which the Americans failed to understand and misunderstood. At one point, Hermann Eilts, who was then a First Secretary in the United States Embassy in London and later, after a distinguished career in the United States Foreign

Service, Director of the School of International Studies at Boston University, signalled to me to join him in the corridor for some urgent discussion. Hermann told me that the Under-Secretary was getting nowhere with his American opposite number, who had just registered alarm at a suggestion that we should employ the "tap on the shoulder approach" towards the governments of the OPEC countries. The Briton understood this expression to mean a friendly approach but, Hermann explained, in the mind of the American it suggested a policeman clapping his hand on the shoulder of a suspect, what the British police call "feeling the collar". I explained to Hermann that our man was so set in his ways and so confident of his negotiating ability that he would not take kindly to being translated as we went along. I suggested that Hermann and I should meet separately after every session to ensure that the two sides had understood each other. Our man returned to London well pleased with himself but expressing disappointment that I had not had much chance to join in the exchanges. I never told him of the private sessions I held with Hermann.

Foreign Office Under Secretaries also exuded confidence in their ability to master exchanges with Americans and oil companies, and in most cases their confidence was justified since they were masters of their political subjects and knew how to explain them in a language understandable to all. But the façade did crack once. As part of the continuing negotiations between OPEC and the companies, the latter had agreed to treat the royalties they paid on a barrel of produced crude oil as an item of current expenditure instead of deducting the amount they had paid in royalties from the eventual profits calculated under the 50-50 agreements. This was known as "expensing of royalties", a concept which one Under Secretary totally failed to grasp, underlining the innumeracy of the pre-war diplomat.

The relations between the OPEC countries and the international oil companies did not change substantially during my three years on the oil desk; nor did those between the companies and the British and American Governments. Great changes were to come later but an account of these belongs in a later part of this narrative.

On our return home from Bahrain in 1961, Christina and I bought a house in Dorking in Surrey from where commuting to London would not be too painful. The demands of my job meant catching the 9.00 a.m. train to London and the 7.00 p.m. train to return to Dorking, a long enough day of about eleven hours, but weekend duty in the Office came rarely. Elizabeth left Monmouth School for Girls to live at home and complete her secondary education at Ewell Technical College and to take a secretarial course at Leatherhead. Robin was now at St John's School at Leatherhead and was able to spend most weekends at home with us. Kathryn was still under school age. There was plenty of scope for outings in the Surrey and Sussex countryside and at the Sussex seaside, and all together the attractions of a settled existence at home became very clear. But the call of duty sounded and in January 1965 Christina, Elizabeth, Kathryn and I were off to Kuwait, where I had been appointed First Secretary, Head of Chancery and Consul at our Embassy.

9

Kuwait

The house into which Christina and I moved in Kuwait was traditionally that occupied by the Assistant Political Agent. Built of mud bricks with an earthen roof, which had to be rolled after the annual rains, and angled and windowed so that the sun never shone directly into the house, it was ideal for the Kuwaiti climate. The ceilings were particularly attractive with red-painted chandals (mangrove poles) below straw matting. It was already a relic of the past since in the late 1950s and early 1960s the Kuwaitis indulged in an orgy of demolition of their old buildings and their replacement with modern structures, sometimes of extraordinary architecture (one house looked, most inappropriately for a Muslim country, like a beer barrel) and of a construction unsuitable for the climate. This unsuitability was relieved by air-conditioning, but the surge in demand for electricity was such that it was many years before Kuwait was able to install sufficient generating capacity to meet peak demands.

This house and the land belonged to the Ruler of Kuwait. Some years later his agent declined to renew the Embassy lease on the grounds that the area was required for development. But when I returned to Kuwait as Ambassador in 1974 I found that no development had taken place and the house had become a Pakistani restaurant, a sad ending for what, for Kuwait, was an historic house. With the wealth that had accrued to the AlSabah one would think that they could have foregone the rent from a Pakistani restaurant in the interests of the history of their State.

Development had proceeded apace since oil wealth began to flow into Kuwait after World War Two. The oil wells had been plugged in 1942 and exploration suspended during the War. Oil exports began in 1946. Kuwait had never been really poor. The autonomous Shaikdom of Kuwait was founded in 1756, following the migration from central Arabia to the shores of the Gulf of some families of the Anaiza tribe. The Head of the AlSabah family was elected as Shaikh and his descendants rule in Kuwait to this day. Kuwait soon became a flourishing port, thanks to the sheltered anchorage provided by its magnificent bay and its fortunate position on trade routes into Arabia. When the Danish explorer, Carsten Niebuhr, visited Kuwait in 1765, he described it as having 10,000 inhabitants and 800 vessels and living by trading, fishing and pearling. Kuwait's commercial fortunes improved further when the East India Company moved the southern terminal of its overland mail route to the Mediterranean from Basra to Kuwait. This was around 1796 when the Persians, at war with Turkey, captured Basra. Much of the Basra trade was diverted to Kuwait. (Two hundred years later the merchants of Kuwait derived similar benefit from the war between Iran and Iraq). Kuwait added shipbuilding to its industry, Kuwaiti dhows and their Kuwaiti sailors becoming famous for the seaworthiness of the former and the seamanship of the latter. Kuwait also became a principal centre for the pearling industry, but this industry was probably the first to suffer, after the incursion of the Japanese cultured pearl, from the more rewarding prospects of employment in the oil industry. Dhow-building also declined, but not so much as pearling since dhows were still required for the intra-Gulf coastal trade. Many of the dhows were now fitted with Kelvin diesel engines, a superbly reliable British product, which helped to make the Kelvin agent in Kuwait very rich indeed. (He later became Lord of the Manor of Wonersh, near Guildford).

    I have already mentioned, in the previous chapter, how British forces came to the aid of Kuwait in 1961. This was not the first time. At the end of the 18th Century the Indian soldiers and warships of the East India Company helped to keep at bay Wahabi raiders from Arabia who sought to impose their interpretation of a fundamentalist Islam on the inhabitants of Kuwait, who were then and have remained tolerant members of the Sunni persuasion, although the resurgence of fundamentalism in the latter half of the 20th Century has forced them to temper their tolerance. Kuwait also benefited from the protection against pirates afforded by the Royal Navy and the Bombay Marine in the 19th Century. In 1899, fearing that the Turks would occupy Kuwait in the wake of their successful support of the house of AlRashid against the future Saudi King, Abdul Aziz Ibn Saud, who fled to Kuwait, the then Shaikh Mubarak turned to the British for protection, signing a treaty which endured until 1961. The Turks tried again in 1900 when a Turkish cruiser carrying troops was seen off by a British cruiser in Kuwait Bay and yet again in 1902 when the Turks established military posts on the approaches to Kuwait. Lord Curzon, Viceroy of India, visited Kuwait in 1903, reaffirmed the treaty of 1899 and appointed, in 1904, the first British Political Agent in Kuwait under the authority of the Political Resident in the Gulf, who at that time had his seat in Bushire, where it had been established by the East India Company in 1788. British forces were again sent to Kuwait in 1919 in response to a Kuwaiti request for help against the Saudi King Ibn Saud who had ordered his Wahabi forces to attack Kuwait. After that episode, including a battle at Jahra below the Matla Ridge where the British troops formed their battle line in 1961, Kuwait lived in peace until the Iraqi threat of 1961. If one expected Kuwait to show some gratitude to Britain for all the political, military and technological effort it had put into making an independent Kuwait safe and wealthy, one would be mistaken, since there is no sense of gratitude in international relations. Britain had therefore to promote its interests in and with Kuwait on the same footing as all the other countries who had discovered Kuwait only in the oil age.

The Ambassador in 1965 was Noel Jackson, who had started his career in the Indian Political Service and had considerable experience of the Gulf. His interests had, however, become centred in horses and he was engaged in writing what proved to be the definitive work on horsemastership. He left the Embassy very much to me and when we held the weekly meeting of the Embassy departments, I took the chair and Noel sat in with the rest of the staff. When he went on leave he would leave me detailed instructions on the care of his horse and his dog. He was a happy man, with an attractive wife, whom he married late, and two small children. But he clearly did not find to his taste modern Kuwait and the 20th Century problems which bedevilled it and Anglo-Kuwaiti relations.

Oil matters loomed large, of course, but at this time relations between the Kuwait Government and the Kuwait Oil Company (KOC), a partnership between BP and Gulf Oil of America, were good. KOC held the concession for Kuwait proper and the American Independent Oil Company (Aminoil), owned by American interests, that for the Kuwaiti share of the Neutral Zone between Saudi Arabia and Kuwait in which each State had "an undivided half-interest." This neat arrangement had been devised by Sir Percy Zachariah Cox, British High Commissioner in Iraq, at a conference at Uqair in 1922, also attended by King Ibn Saud, at which the frontiers of Iraq, Kuwait and Saudi Arabia were defined. The concessionaire for the offshore area of the Neutral Zone was the Japanese-owned Arabian Oil Company; and the Kuwait Shell Petroleum Development Company (a wholly owned subsidiary of the Royal Dutch Shell Group) was awarded in 1960 a concession for the offshore area of Kuwait. This award soon ran into protests from Iran, Iraq and Saudi Arabia, who, since the seabed boundaries in the northern Gulf had not been defined, felt that their interests were threatened. One of my first tasks on arriving in Kuwait was to attend a National Assembly debate at which the Kuwait Government informed the Assembly that it would have to respect the protests of its neighbours and place the Shell concession in moratorium.

Our heavy baggage from the United Kingdom had been sent by sea and wrongly offloaded at Khorramshahr. It eventually arrived at our house on a Thursday in April, three months after we had arrived, and Christina and I spent a happy weekend unpacking and placing our personal possessions around the house. I found that my Distinguished Flying Cross was missing along with my MBE and other decorations and my diplomatic uniform hat and boots. Somewhere between Dorking and Kuwait somebody had got into the packing case, ripped open the bottom of my tin uniform case and removed these articles, which, no doubt, afforded the thief some amusement from the hat, dry and comfortable feet from the boots, and some profit from the decorations. But the house now looked as much like home as we could make it and we looked forward to enjoying it for the next two or three years. But when I went to the Embassy on the Saturday morning (Friday being the local day of rest) I found a telegram from the Foreign Office instructing me to proceed on promotion to Counsellor (Diplomatic Service Grade 4) as

British Political Agent in Abu Dhabi, which Christina and I had last visited in 1960. So I had to tell Christina to start packing again.

Noel Jackson was not pleased by this instruction from London since the Embassy had recently been inspected and he was hoping that the Diplomatic Service Inspectors would recommend the abolition of the Economic Counsellor's post and the upgrading of the Head of Chancery to Counsellor with me in that job. He tried to persuade me to turn down Abu Dhabi but I pointed out to him the confidence which the Political Resident and the Foreign Office had shown in me not to mention the attraction of one's own command, however small. He did, however, have my services for a further two months for reasons connected with the Political Agent's house which Sir William Luce, the Political Resident, explained to Christina and me when we visited Bahrain in May.

10

Political Agent in Abu Dhabi

On 16 July 1965 my wife Christina, our six-year-old daughter Kathryn and I arrived in the sweltering summer heat of the Persian Gulf Shaikhdom of Abu Dhabi, one of the Trucial States, where I had been appointed as the British Political Agent. Under the Treaties of Perpetual Peace, which the Rulers of the Gulf Shaikhdoms of Kuwait, Bahrain, Qatar and the Trucial States had signed with the British Government since 1820, and which gave Britain a Special Position in the Gulf excluding all other foreign representation, a Political Agent was at once a British diplomatic representative and an adviser on external affairs and defence to the Ruler to whom he was accredited. Inevitably, in playing his part in promoting the traditional British foreign policy of enlightened self-interest, a Political Agent became involved in advising the Ruler on internal affairs as these impacted on the wider world in which both British and Shaikhly Governments had to make their way, sometimes separately, sometimes together.

The Political Agent I was succeeding was Colonel Hugh (later Sir Hugh) Boustead CMG DSO MC and Bar, a colourful character who was said to have deserted from the Royal Navy during the First World War to see action with the Army, in which he was a Captain with an MC before the Navy caught up with him. After the war Hugh joined the Sudan Civil Service, served with forces in East Africa during the Second World War, back to the Sudan and on to East Aden Protectorate after that war. Before his appointment to Abu Dhabi in 1962 he had been British Agent and Resident Adviser in the Hadhramaut States. After a lifetime of commanding, advising and guiding in the Arab World (and not expecting any disagreement) Hugh had become rather "shaikhly" himself, affecting a camel stick and a whistle with which he summoned his bearer and other retainers. The Assistant Political Agent in Abu Dhabi, Duncan Slater, also a former

RAF pilot, and later an Under Secretary in the Foreign Office and Ambassador to Oman, told me that he always expected to be told by Hugh that a certain blast on the whistle would mean that he, Duncan, should come running. Hugh was not at all house or office trained and tended to disrupt proceedings: for example, scattering confidential papers from the FO Diplomatic Bag around his house for Duncan to locate and gather for filing and action. Lady Luce, the wife of Sir William Luce, the Political Resident in the Gulf from 1962 to 1966, remarked in her book *From Aden to the Gulf* that when she and the Political Resident set off with Christina and me on a visit to the Liwa Oasis in 1966 there were differences, "perhaps the greatest is to be without Hugh, as all our Liwa expeditions had been with him. This may have meant that the expedition set off in a rather smoother way but I missed the shouting and the confusion". Sir William told me that Hugh had been sent to Abu Dhabi because he was "good with Arabs"; but he had got nowhere with the Ruler of Abu Dhabi and had probably reached the age (he was over 70) when he should have retired. Later I came to know that he had not got on with the Ruler because the latter felt that there should be only one Shaikh, himself, in Abu Dhabi and he resented Hugh's "shaikhly" attitude. Also, Hugh probably came up against, for the first time, an "Arab" who would not do what Hugh told him. Hugh was a late member of a generation of Arab experts referred to in a Foreign Office document preserved in the files of the Public Record Office and quoted by Sir James Craig in his book *Shemlan: A History of the Middle East Centre for Arab Studies:* "Colonel Bertram Thomas is representative of a generation of Arab experts whose influence and intimate knowledge of Middle Eastern affairs is fast vanishing. He and his period of Arab experts acquired their knowledge of the Arabs and the Arab World at a time when bedouin life and the tribal outlook was all important". New imperatives informed Abu Dhabi from the 1950s. (And now I am of a later generation whose Arab expertise is out of date and must defer to the generation represented by my son, Robin, HM Ambassador-designate to the Kingdom of Bahrain).

Hugh left me three legacies I could have done without. He had wrecked the Agency launch required for visiting ships at anchor offshore; there was no dock or quay in 1960s Abu Dhabi. I had to hire a launch whenever my duties demanded a visit, in diplomatic uniform in the case of the Royal Navy, to ships. The second legacy was six .303 Lee-Enfield rifles which he had stored for the defence of the Agency if the need should arise. Rifles were not at all approved equipment for a British diplomatic post and I got rid of them to the Trucial Oman Scouts.

Sir William Luce communicated the third legacy to Christina and me when we visited Bahrain to be briefed by him on the prospect before us. "Before coming to your task in Abu Dhabi," said Sir William, "there is another problem: the house in which you will have to live. Only bachelor political Officers and Hugh Boustead have occupied it and under Hugh's reign it has become known as 'Dysentery Hall'. It is not suitable for a family and I want you to pay an advance visit to Abu Dhabi so that Christina may see what will be required to make it family-friendly".

We paid our visit, at the same time calling on Shaikh Shakhbut, the Ruler, who greeted us with the courtesy and kindness he always showed towards us. Christina saw that not much could be done to the house apart from giving it, including the greasy kitchen (described by a visiting Diplomatic Service Inspector as "deplorable"), a good clean, since the construction of the house was odd. On the ground floor were three bedrooms open to the desert and into which the odd traveller, told by Hugh to make himself at home, would, to use a Hugh expression, "throw his boots". An outside staircase led to the first floor where, off a verandah, were found the sitting and dining rooms, a small bedroom and the kitchen. That was it. Christina asked for a "purdah" wall to be built outside the ground floor bedrooms to provide some privacy, for a front door to be included in the wall, and for an additional bedroom and bathroom on the ground floor for Kathryn's governess: there was, of course, no school in Abu Dhabi, of which more later. All this was agreed to without argument, the Foreign Office and the Ministry of Works being equally appalled at the thought of the Lamb family living in the house as it stood. The only work which went wrong was that the roof of the governess's room was sloped *into* the end wall of the house with the result that when heavy rain fell soon after our arrival, water poured down the inside wall onto her bed. This seemingly impossible-for-a-builder-to-make blunder was soon corrected. The Ministry of Works was represented in Abu Dhabi by a lowly but willing clerk of works who, whenever we asked him what he would do about a problem within his competence would reply "Nothing; I'll do something", which well matched the "Up a bit lower" advised by a dart player in the Sergeants' Mess at Thornhill in Southern Rhodesia when I was a pupil pilot there in 1941. Later we enclosed one end of the verandah for a small sitting-room for Christina when I entertained Shaikhs and other Arab notables in the sitting room and dining room. Until we had that room - and tiny it was - Christina had to retire to her bedroom on such occasions.

After Sir William had dealt with the problem of the house he went on to brief me on the political and diplomatic task before me and of which he reminded me in a despatch of 23 October 1965 (my 44th Birthday) after I was *en poste*, that HMG were concerned "over Shaikh Shakhbut's reactionary attitude to the progress and development of his State...your objective, particularly in view of the expected rapid increase in his income from oil, must be to bring the Ruler to realise that he cannot continue policies more suited to past centuries than to the present years. The outcome of your efforts will be important in the context of the future stability and development of the Trucial States as a whole". This message was underlined in a Foreign Office Minute by the Permanent Under-Secretary, Sir Paul Gore-Booth, who, having read my First Impressions Despatch (a Foreign Office tradition) commented:

> *This is a most vivid description of an interesting personality and a difficult situation. But I think we must really pull up the author on one point. He says, "Her Majesty's Government will suffer <u>no more than</u> (my underlining) criticism for tolerating such a state of affairs." Surely we ought to make it clear, even in advance of the Defence Review that this is not at all the perspective in which H. M. Government see this situation. They see themselves pledged to a somewhat more rapid advancement in the Gulf than has taken place hitherto and, quite apart from their own wishes, the time is moving very fast and our own position may well depend on our ability to promote and guide that advance. A failure to do so might well result in much more than "criticism".*

Thus was my task in Abu Dhabi made clear to me. But why were we trying so late in the 20th Century to bring Shaikh Shakhbut into it; and why was it so difficult to do? Who was Shaikh Shakhbut, and what had made him what he was?

Shaikh Shakhbut bin Sultan AlNahayyan succeeded his murdered father in 1928. Murder had been a common practice in the family and many said it was a miracle that Shakhbut survived. But his strong-minded mother made his brothers swear that they would support and safeguard Shakhbut. Abu Dhabi was a truly impoverished shaikhdom, the fishing and pearling, which had once sustained the Abu Dhabians on the coast, had declined to near invisibility and agriculture in the Buraimi Oasis never rose above subsistence level. Shakhbut's mother was said to keep a carpet, once her sole possession, to remind the family how poor they had once been. Her sons were devoted to her and one or more of them would call on her every day.

A tradition of poverty had understandably made Shaikh Shakhbut careful with money, just like his neighbour the Sultan of Muscat and Oman. Also like the Sultan, Shaikh Shakhbut would not spend money when he had it. He kept large sums of money in notes in his Palace. Inevitably some of it disappeared from time to time to the fury of Shaikh Shakhbut, who never seemed to suspect his two dissolute sons, Said and Sultan, both of whom died young. In her book, *From Aden to the Gulf,* Lady Luce recalls the atmosphere in the Palace when she and the Political Resident called on Shaikh Shakhbut shortly after he had discovered that £22,000 had been stolen from his safe: Shakhbut had one of his apoplectic rages. I doubt that anyone, except his two sons, who knew where his hoard was kept, would dare to steal it. When, occasionally, the Political Agency paid a bill for him he would send a suitcase of notes to meet his debt. He was always punctilious in money matters with the Agency but not with others, especially if he did not approve of the goods or services they had delivered to him.

This insistence on value (as he saw it) for money produced Abu Dhabi's own Clochemerle story. Shaikh Shakhbut suddenly accepted that times had changed: no longer should his people use the beach at Abu Dhabi as a lavatory. He commissioned a young Lebanese to build public toilets along the beach, simple concrete block constructions projecting over the water with a hole in the floor, which would be cleaned by the tides. The toilets were built but the people ignored them and continued to use the beach. Shaikh Shakhbut refused to pay the bill, blaming the Lebanese for building toilets that his people would not use. He clapped the unfortunate young man (as an Arab he came under the Ruler's jurisdiction; all other nationalities came under HMG's, administered by the Political Agent) into prison but eventually let him go, the toilets remaining as proof, Shaikh Shakbut informed me, that his people did not want progress. In the same context he said to me one day "My people have been without a hospital for a thousand years and are healthy. Why should they need a hospital now?"

Shaikh Shakhbut had indeed been prevailed upon some years earlier to buy a prefabricated hospital but refused to have it erected, maintaining that the suppliers should have put it up. The rights and wrongs of the contract between the Ruler and the supplier were never cleared up and the prefabricated sections of the hospital lay in the desert increasingly disappearing from view under the blowing sand. The oil companies operating in Abu Dhabi were self-contained for medical services; but the rest of us had no hospital, no clinic, no pharmacy, no dentist and just one eccentric Irish doctor, Desmond McCaully, who had come to Abu Dhabi in the mid-1960s after an ungrateful Dubai, where he had practised for years, told him to leave. He was a sad, lonely character whose wife, he told me more than once, had been stolen by another man; but the enormity of this man's offence had been compounded by his also stealing the doctor's golf clubs. Julian Walker also remembers Dr McCaully with obvious affection in his book *Tyro on the Trucial Coast:* "Warm-hearted, hospitable, and conscientious in his profession but not one of its most brilliant shooting stars. A magnificent drinker". We all did our best to stay healthy; but when our daughter Kathryn became unwell Christina had to take her to Bahrain for diagnosis and treatment.

Christina, Kathryn and I had a rather adventurous flight from Bahrain to Abu Dhabi in a twin-engine de Havilland Dove.

As we approached the latter the visibility deteriorated markedly and was down to 500 feet when we arrived over the landing-strip. The pilot had almost decided to over-fly Abu Dhabi and divert to Dubai when the airstrip loomed up in front of us, the pilot cut the engines and down we bumped. Where we landed the aircraft was quite invisible from the ground. The reception party was somewhat perturbed when they heard the engines cut out and did not see the aircraft until it trundled along in front of them out of the murk. On the Ruler's instructions we were met by a guard of honour of 24 Abu Dhabi policemen commanded by Shaikh Mubarak bin Mohamed.

The next morning Duncan Slater and I were preparing to put on our uniforms to call on the Ruler when I received a telephone call from him to say that he wished to call on me. I said that I should have the honour of calling on him first since this was the correct protocol. He replied that he wanted friendship not protocol and was going to call on me whatever my preference. I received him in my house, made much of the honour he was signally doing me and we had a most friendly talk. He repeated what he had said when Christina and I called on him in May about his pleasure in seeing me and how, together, we should see Abu Dhabi grow and prosper. He expressed again his delight in having a married Political Agent and chatted happily to Christina and to six-year-old Kathryn. He asked Kathryn if she preferred Kuwait or Abu Dhabi; we held our breath but the young diplomat replied without hesitation "Abu Dhabi". This made Shaikh Shakhbut laugh, as did her further reply when he asked her why she liked Abu Dhabi: she replied, "Because it is more exciting".

Our house was now beginning to respond to improvements, the *purdah* screen outside the bedrooms on the ground floor had been completed as well as the two extra bedrooms. Unfortunately the air conditioning on the first floor was almost completely nullified by the odd siting of the conditioning units – at floor level in the very corners of the two living rooms. Thus the furniture interfered with the circulation of the cooling air, which eventually found its way across the floor and out without having cooled anything except our feet and ankles. I asked the Ministry of Works (in those days solely responsible for Foreign

Office property overseas) to move the units up to window openings which existed and which were large enough to take the units (for which I suspected they had been installed) only to receive a rather silly reply saying that to do so would be "contrary to Departmental Practice", which was presumably based on a theory peculiar to the Ministry of Works that cold air rises and warm air falls.

Eventually, but only after further pressure from me and from the Political Residency in Bahrain, the MoW agreed that the correct placing for the units was on high. But among the expatriate population of Abu Dhabi the reputation of the Political Agency remained that it was the hottest house in the town. We, and our guests, perspired or glowed gently according to sex.

Christina paid her courtesy call on the Ruler's only wife, Shaikha Mariam, who, Christina found, was much younger than her husband and very pretty despite her *betula* (facemask), with a gentle voice and a keen interest in current affairs, especially in education. Shaikha Mariam had a television set on which she said she could receive programmes from Dhahran in Saudi Arabia and Kuwait. Christina gradually called on other women of the Ruling Family, including the Ruler's mother, Shaikha Salamah bint Butti, Shaikha Fatima, the senior and favourite wife of Shaikh Zayid, and other ladies of the Ruling Family whenever we visited Buraimi where all of them lived.

During my tour of duty in the Political Residency in Bahrain from 1957 to 1961 I had several opportunities to visit Abu Dhabi and to make the acquaintance of Shaikh Shakhbut, other members of his family and the merchants, of whom there was only a handful of pitifully low standard. Now that I was *en poste* in Abu Dhabi and in touch daily with Ruler, his family and the merchants I found that nothing in Abu Dhabi had changed in four years. The town was still a shanty town and a shambles. There were some new buildings: three British-owned banks, two of them in grandiose premises; a barracks for a non-existent army; and a power station yet unconnected to a distribution system. A prefabricated hospital still lay in packing cases in the desert two years after delivery. The only successful project, for which the Ruler had to be given credit, was a sweet water pipeline from wells some 80 miles to the east of Abu Dhabi town. Otherwise Abu Dhabi remained undeveloped or, as the Ruler would have it, unspoiled. The merchants had improved slightly in quality and their number had increased; but the economic stagnation had denied them opportunities to flourish and widen their trading experience.

The lack of development was not due to lack of money: increasing oil production from two oil fields, one on land and one offshore, provided sufficient revenues to finance a development programme suited to the needs of this sparsely-populated Shaikhdom. Nor was it due to the reluctance of Abu Dhabians as a whole to see their traditional way of life change: they looked with envy to Kuwait, Bahrain, Qatar and also to Dubai, oil-less but pulling itself up by its bootstraps under the commonsense leadership of its Ruler, Shaikh Rashid AlMaktum. The only obstacle to the development of Abu Dhabi was the Ruler, Shaikh Shakhbut, to whom wealth had come only very recently.

Shaikh Shakhbut was in 1965 about 60 years of age, a small frail-looking man who dressed and lived simply. He had much charm when he decided to use it and a good sense of humour. He was tolerant of the social and religious habits of non-Muslims. He had tremendous self-confidence but a total inability to trust others. The first of these two latter characteristics enabled him to be certain that his opinion was always the correct one and to have no fear for his own personal safety: he must have been the most unguarded Ruler in the Arab World, frequently taking motor-car trips around Abu Dhabi Island accompanied only by his driver; and never having a crowd of armed retainers in his *majlis*, where everybody who requested an audience was admitted.

His second characteristic – his lack of trust – was a failing for which I felt sorry for him. I tried to think what my own life would be if I could not trust anyone to play fair with me. This failing made him instantly suspicious, where the expenditure of money was concerned, of everyone's motives and interests and, regrettably, made him very receptive of hints that he was being "cheated, betrayed and played around with", to use one of his comments soon after my arrival. It also made him a ready prey for any second-rate contractor or entrepreneur who claimed that he could do a job on the cheap; and confirmed the Ruler in his belief, when the second-rate job proved a non-starter or a failure, that every businessman was out to rob him.

Shaikh Shakhbut was still living in a world that had been familiar to him for his entire 60 years where every rupee counted. This might be considered to his credit since he was unlikely to countenance any gross waste of public funds as occurred, for example, in Saudi Arabia; but it also restricted severely his understanding of true values and costs in the world of the mid-Twentieth Century. An example of this lack of understanding (I doubt that it was "meanness" in the accepted sense of the word) occurred immediately after he had signed, on 19 September 1965, the Income Tax Law which gave effect to the 50/50 Agreements with the two oil companies, Abu Dhabi Marine Areas (ADMA) and Abu Dhabi Petroleum Company (ADPC), and would bring him and estimated income of around £30 million over the following twelve months – for a State of 25,000 people: he asked me the cost of employing the services of two British Army officers; when I told him he declared that it was too much and that he could not possibly afford it.

The Ruler's family were aware of his failings but were powerless to correct them. They all lived in awe of him and were completely dependent upon him for their livelihood. None of them had a fixed income (there was no such thing as a Civil List) and they feared to upset him lest they lost the occasional handout. His own two sons, Said and Sultan, would contribute little or probably nothing to Abu Dhabi's progress even if Shaikh Shakhbut embraced development and a suitable supporting administration. Sultan was corrupt, feckless and unpopular whilst Said, diabetic and not quite normal (his hysterical laughter at the weakest jokes was alarming on first acquaintance) was popular with the *bedu,* and a regular subvention and permission to spend all his time in Buraimi would have helped his father with the tribes. Their cousins, the sons of Shaikh Muhammad bin Khalifa AlNahayyan, the Ruler's first cousin, were, on the contrary, intelligent and purposeful, even if uneducated, but unfortunately limited by their financial dependence on Shaikh Shakhbut. They were to come into their own after Shaikh Zayid became Ruler. But in 1965 the latter, then Governor of the Buraimi Oasis, told me firmly that he would not go against his brother, Shaikh Shakhbut having warned him never to contradict or question his decisions. I received much advice from Shaikh Zayid on how to handle his brother and on many other subjects: for example, on the raising of children, the importance to them of regular habits and rest while at the same time his own young children wandered around at all hours. I thought that this contradiction between theory and practice could mean that he might not always be submissive to Shaikh Shakhbut if the AlNahayyan control of Abu Dhabi were to be threatened by the Ruler's intransigence. Indeed Shaikh Zayid did begin to urge upon the Ruler the wisdom of administrative progress.

Thus in carrying out my instructions from the Political Resident I could deal only with Shaikh Shakhbut, absolute Ruler and only fount of wealth and wisdom. But the mechanism that controlled the fountain was out of order, or at best erratic, the wealth did not flow and the wisdom was sadly lacking in recognising the essential need of development. On external affairs Shaikh Shakhbut was sensible and cooperative, showing no lack of trust in Her Majesty's Government: one could say, cynically, that this was only because HMG's conduct of his external relations cost him nothing; and their protection permitted him to do what he liked internally. His conviction that all actions were dictated by the perpetrator's self-interest would certainly have led him to the conclusion that HMG would not have afforded him their protection unless it was in their interests to do so. So his lamentable conduct of internal affairs continued while HMG protected him and became identified with his refusal to move into the 20th Century. There could be no doubt that if he continued his maladministration the outlook for Abu Dhabi and for HMG was bleak. The people of Abu Dhabi, including the tribes whom Shaikh Zayid was finding increasingly difficult to control, were restive and it was not out of the question that one day, if the Ruler did not change his ways, they would revolt against him. Meanwhile HMG had to continue to use "cajolery and persuasion", as a visiting journalist described the British approach to Shaikh Shakhbut. We had no sanctions we could use against him and could only go on trying through words to persuade him into essential reforms. While such a task might be unrewarding I found it amusing and exhilarating, if at times annoying, since the Ruler, who had my affection if not my admiration, was always prepared to argue his case even if it lacked logic or was based on a false premise, making, except to him, a nonsense of his argument.

I was optimistic – I had to be! - that the sheer pressure of the wealth flowing from the oilfields would persuade him into setting up an administration to manage that wealth. My first priority was to help him to make that move forward. Since a gross waste of public funds was unimaginable under Shaikh Shakhbut, the essential basic development of his State would not absorb more than a small part of the State's accruing wealth. But before any of this future could be realised the Ruler would have to delegate some responsibility to competent officials; but this eventually proved impossible: nothing could surmount Shaikh Shakhbut's total inability to trust anyone he employed; and there was no development in Abu Dhabi while he remained Ruler.

When Shaikh Shakhbut died in 1989 at the age of 83, his obituary in *The Times* said that he had refused a £25 million development project. I do not recall this but it is always possible that some visitor to his majlis broached such grandiose expenditure. The highest capital expenditure I discussed with him was for £500,000 (about £5 million in 2002 money). With such modest expenditure Abu Dhabi could have had the erection of the prefabricated hospital which lay in the desert increasingly covered from view by the blowing sand, schools, some roads and some other items of essential infrastructure sufficient for the small population, estimated by the Political Agency with the assistance of the Trucial Oman Scouts to be not more than 25,000 in the whole territory of some 25,000 square miles – about the size of Wales. Shaikh Shakhbut did not, therefore, need to spend millions, which was not only above the absorptive capacity of his Shaikhdom but would also attract too many outsiders to Abu Dhabi with the risk of overwhelming the native inhabitants.

In October 1965 the Political Resident discussed with Shaikh Shakhbut the question of government organisation in Abu Dhabi and recommended the acceptance of, and early action on, proposals I would be putting to him at his, the Ruler's, request. Perhaps encouraged by and responding to Sir William's words, Shaikh Shakhbut paid his staff-for the first time in three months. All payments were made in cash and the total sum expended was £60,000: thus the interesting fact emerged that the administration of Abu Dhabi cost £20,000 per month. When signing the cheque to draw the money from the bank, Shakhbut commented grimly that he did not seem to be getting much for all this money; and that surely the United States Government would not cost more! Having disposed of these affairs of state, Shaikh Shakhbut decided, for the first time in three years, to buy new shoes. A retainer was despatched to the only shop selling shoes and returned with two pairs costing a total of about £5.00. The disbursement of so much money all in one morning was too much for him and sent him into a long tirade about the extent to which he was being overcharged in all directions. He let it be known that it would be some months before his staff were paid again.

This episode reminded us yet again of the problem presented by the Ruler, and him alone, in persuading him to face up to the world which was to come whether he wanted it or not. It appeared that he had no intention of lying back and enjoying it. But I went ahead and presented to the Ruler a memorandum covering the proposals for government organisation, reminding him of his conversation with the Political Resident. He thanked me and promised to discuss the subject further with me. In the memorandum I recommended a Ruler's Office, an Advisory Council, a Controller-General (a sort of Permanent Under Secretary) to oversee the creation and development of government departments as required, a financial control system, budgetary arrangements and a modest development programme. The Ruler and I returned to the subject later and I was surprised but pleased when he said that he had no questions, everything was clear and that the recommendations, all of which he accepted, he saw were in the interests of Abu Dhabi. But (there was always a "but") the establishment of an administration would require as a first step the building of houses and offices for the officials. He was therefore going to submit my proposals to his engineers for the calculation of the cost of such accommodation. Yet again Shaikh Shakhbut had seized on a detail to put off coming to grips with the wider issues. We continued our exchanges about administration and financial control whenever we met and at one time he seemed to be ready to appoint a Director of Finance; but once again he shied away from any decision.

At the same time he had agreed to distribute to contractors tender documents prepared by a firm of British consulting engineers for road-building, saying with apparent sincerity that he wished to push on with the development projects which were so important for Abu Dhabi. The Political Resident and I continued to try our best to persuade him into the paths of virtue seen not only by HMG and its Representatives but also by members of the AlNahayyan, principally the Ruler's two brothers, Shaikh Zayid and Shaikh Khalid, who lent their best efforts to the task of persuading Shaikh Shakhbut to accept the proposals we had made to him. We all failed. In August 1965 he terminated his agreement with the British consulting engineers on the abundantly false grounds that their specifications were useless; and cancelled all development projects. Later he agreed to the erection of the pre-fabricated hospital; but changed his mind again about that and about ordering equipment for the hospital. Similarly with the formation of an administration and the formulation of a budget, no progress was made.

Outside his own domain he snubbed his fellow Rulers on the Trucial States Council (the forerunner of the United Arab Emirates) by refusing to attend or send representatives to meetings of the Council and its committees, or to agree to Trucial States-wide laws and regulations welcomed by the six other Rulers; and refused to attend the Council's meetings with other Gulf Rulers.

Despite his difficult nature Shaikh Shakhbut had, as I have already recorded, my affection, but not my admiration, since he could not see that the only enemy he had was himself. He was always unpredictable, not only in the reasons he gave for opposing ideas and proposals but in the way he expressed that opposition. When I had to inform him of HMG's ruling, which he had agreed should be made but which did not go his way, on the seabed boundary between Abu Dhabi and Dubai, a ruling made essential by the development of the oil industry, on shore and offshore; he went positively berserk and beat everyone in the *majlis* (with the exception of the Political Agent) with his camel stick.

Meanwhile the two oil companies operating in Abu Dhabi, ADMA and the ADPC, continued to produce and search for oil and to contribute ever-increasing revenues to the State of Abu Dhabi. Only one cloud appeared in their operational sky during my time in the Shaikhdom. Towards the end of 1965 the Arab labour employed by ADMA on Das Island demanded the introduction of a system of working three weeks on and one week off which ADPC practised on the mainland. Showing bland insouciance if not industrial innocence, Shaikh Hamdan bin Mohamed, the Ruler's representative on the Island, instructed the labour not to press their demand until he returned from a hunting holiday in Oman when he would deal with it. ADMA was not unduly alarmed by the situation, going ahead with a visit to the Island by the Abu Dhabi cricket team accompanied by wives and children. However, on the day of the match five ringleaders emerged from the Arab workers and persuaded the latter to strike from 11 December. When I returned to Abu Dhabi on 10 December from a visit to Bahrain I was informed that two ADMA helicopters were on their way to the mainland to take a detachment of Trucial Oman Scouts to the Island. I immediately sent a signal to the TOS commander ordering him not to send troops to the Island but the aircraft were already in the air. It emerged that a British officer in the still embryo Abu Dhabi Defence Force (ADDF) who was a member of the visiting cricket team had taken upon himself, without any authority, to persuade the OC TOS, also acting too hastily without any authority to place any of his force under a foreign flag, to place 16 Scouts under his command. The important first priority would have been to get a member of the Ruling Family to the Island immediately but the ADMA General manager and the over-enthusiastic ADDF officer did not think of this. All the senior male members of the Ruling Family, including the Ruler, were away hunting in Oman, except for Sultan bin Shakhbut who was fishing offshore Abu Dhabi. I was able to contact him and he obtained his father's authority to go to Das and to deliver a message from the Ruler asking the strikers to let him know their demands for discussion with the company. Meanwhile I cancelled a further unauthorised delivery of TOS to the Island. ADMA's General Manager expressed his disappointment at this decision when I informed him by telephone; but since he saw no need to evacuate the cricket party I remained convinced that the situation on the Island was being over-dramatised and not thought out. I was also worried about the legal position of the Scouts under the unauthorised command of the ADDF officer and the complications which might follow from their precipitate use. I persuaded the OC TOS to accompany me to Das and to take over the command of his scouts, which he should never have surrendered to an agent of the Abu Dhabi Government.

When I arrived at the airport for my flight to Das Sultan told me that the Ruler had changed his mind: he (Sultan) was not to go to Das; a Palestinian named Salim Ali Moussa would take the Ruler's message to the strikers. Sultan refused to accompany me so I flew to Das with the OC TOS and Salim. He took the Ruler's message to the workers who rejected it out of hand. Then Sultan arrived full of apologies for misunderstanding his father's instructions. Sultan was accompanied, on the Ruler's instructions, by a senior member of the Ruling Family and the Imam of the Friday Mosque in Abu Dhabi. These three spoke to the strikers, who eventually agreed to await the return of Shaikh Hamdan. Meanwhile the Scouts, whose presence had irritated the workers, were returned to their base on the mainland.

It was understandable that the General Manager should have been concerned at the possibility of trouble on his tiny island; but there appeared to have been no calming voice among his staff, only one of whom had sufficient Arabic to establish meaningful contact with the workers, and who appear to have thrown up their hands when Shaikh Hamdan could not be found. No consideration had been given to informing the Political Agent and/or asking for another member of the Ruling Family to visit the Island; but immediate recourse to the British ADDF officer on the safeguarding of life and limb, to which there was no threat. A politically inept performance which ignored both the immediate responsibility of the Abu Dhabi Government and the wider responsibility of HMG. The former might reasonably have been asked to reinforce the Abu Dhabi police presence on the Island. In addition to the workers' resentment at the presence of TOS on the Island the Ruler also took umbrage, complaining to me about their presence without consultation with him. Eventually the workers' grievances were redressed after further contacts between their representatives and the Ruler, who was forced by the absence of Shaikh Hamdan and the incompetence of Shaikh Sultan to deal directly with the problem.

Of a different calibre to the other members of the Ruling Family was Shaikh Zayid bin Sultan, fourth and youngest son, born about 1916, of Shaikha Salamah bint Butti. Shaikh Zayid, who had wider, grander ideas than his brother Shakhbut for the future of Abu Dhabi, embodied everyone's idea of a desert shaikh. Tall, firm featured and hook-nosed, more robustly built than the slight and delicately-featured Shakhbut, with a swagger that suggested that the wind of heaven was blowing through his *bisht* (Arab cloak), Shaikh Zayid was the man the Ruling Family and the people of Abu Dhabi, not to mention the British Government, hoped might persuade his brother to open the moneybags – metaphorically, not literally, since Shaikh Shakhbut did not keep his wealth "in notes stacked in petrol tins" as *The Times* obituary would have it. Shaikh Zayid spoke well on the topic of persuading his brother to spend more money whenever it was raised with him but it was important for me to remember that for the Arab, especially the *bedu*, to whom Zayid's way of life was close, words are an art form and words spoken can mean deeds done.

Shaikh Zayid had little formal education but this did not prevent his establishing himself as an able and percipient administrator in the Buraimi area where he was for many years the Ruler's representative. Despite a constant shortage of funds he brought considerable development to the Buraimi area. Frequently frustrated and irritated by the Ruler's eccentric behaviour he remained loyal to his brother. When I first met him at Buraimi in July 1965 I was immediately impressed although we did not discuss affairs of state at all but confined ourselves to family chat. My being married with a semi-grown-up family (he had his two sons Sultan and Hamdan with him) commended me to him especially, said Zayid, because we were of the same age, although he might be a year or two younger! He tried to persuade me to learn to ride but after I had had a look at his horses I decided not to get on their backs. Fortunately he did not press me on this.

Shaikh Zayid was consistently resolute in defence of Abu Dhabi's interests against the long-standing claims of the Saudi Arabian Government to considerable areas of Abu Dhabi territory where oil had been discovered. In February 1966 HMG informed the Saudi Arabian Government of its obligations to the Rulers of the Trucial States, obligations which it intended to honour. I informed Shaikh Shakhbut that this statement covered his problems with the Saudis. A few months after Shaikh Zayid took over as Ruler of Abu Dhabi he visited Riyadh to pay his respects to King Faisal of Saudi Arabia, who presented him with a renewed claim to Abu Dhabi territory covering the recently-discovered oilfields. Zayid temporised, returned to Abu Dhabi and, certainly during my time in Abu Dhabi, never replied to King Faisal's claim. The history of the Saudi claim to Abu Dhabi territory is beyond the scope of this memoir.

Occasionally his frustration with Shaikh Shakhbut would bring him to call on me or take me into a quiet corner of his Buraimi palace to unburden himself. He would complain that his brother was not amenable to reason. Both he and Shaikh Khalid had tried their best but to no avail and only by frightening him would HMG be able to bring him to his senses. I would point out that HMG were responsible for the defence and external affairs of Abu Dhabi but had no authority to direct the Ruler on how to govern his shaikhdom. The responsibility lay with the AlNahayyan.

Shaikh Khalid bin Sultan would also call on me occasionally to vent his anger with his brother. Where Zayid was reasonable and mild in his criticism, choosing his words carefully, Khalid would always be unashamedly intemperate in his language. He would tell me that I should place no faith in the sweet words of Shakhbut about his intention to form an administration, press on with development projects and rely on the advice and assistance of HMG. He and Zayid thought that they had persuaded Shakhbut to ask HMG for a Briton as Director of Finance; but since Shakhbut knew that he could not "play around with" a British official seconded by HMG he set such terms for the appointment that HMG would be unable to find anyone to accept them. Shakhbut was determined to keep everything in his own hands. Shakhbut might listen to the advice of Zayid, Khalid and their cousin Mohamed bin Khalifah, the senior member of the Family after Shakhbut, but he would either reject it outright or find a way to avoid taking it. To Khalid, too, I had to say that the solution lay with the AlNahayyan.

Eventually the Family found a solution and accepted their responsibility.

Christina, Kathryn and I went home on leave in the summer of 1966 after 18 months in the Gulf (we had served six months in the Embassy in Kuwait before moving to Abu Dhabi). Before we went Shaikh Zayid told me that he would be visiting Britain and would be staying at a house called Hall Barn in Beaconsfield which had been taken for him by the Eastern Bank, one of the three banks in Abu Dhabi (the other two were the British Bank of the Middle East and the Ottoman Bank) ever hopeful of profitable times to come. When I called on Shaikh Zayid at Hall Barn he told me, after we had discussed the shortcomings of Shaikh Shakhbut, that the Ruling Family with himself in the lead would move against Shaikh Shakhbut if the latter would not change his ways, and replace him. So it happened in early August 1966 as described by Glen Balfour-Paul, then Acting Political Resident in the Gulf, in Gerald Butt's book *The Lion in the Sand*:

> *I knew Shaikh Shakhbut well and liked him a lot. But during an interim between two Political Residents the present Ruler of Abu Dhabi, Shaikh Zaid, came to see me after visiting London. He told me that he and his family wished to have a change of Ruler because of Shakhbut's notorious meanness or wisdom, depending on whether you think that spending vast sums of money on welfare was for the benefit of the people or not. But, anyhow, Shaikh*

> Zaid decided he must go, and all his family wanted him to go. He wasn't prepared to do it himself because they were all very frightened of Shakhbut. So I had to go down (i.e. from Bahrain to Abu Dhabi) and visit the Ruler in his isolated fort in what then was desert and tell him we wished him to retire with dignity and so on. He got very, very angry indeed and shut all the doors and sent his retainers up onto the roof with their muskets, and they were carrying ammunition up and down stairs – it was quite a dramatic time. I was quite glad to get out of the Palace after an hour or two, and it took several hours in the afternoon to eventually persuade him as decently as we could to come out. We had some Trucial Scouts hidden around the Palace but they were not to intervene unless the balloon went up. Appeals were made to his retainers to come out and some of them came without shots being fired. In the end he emerged, there was a guard of honour, and it was all done with as much dignity as possible.

I was recalled from leave to return to Abu Dhabi to make my number with the new Ruler and to ensure that all was for the best for Abu Dhabi and for HMG. It was.

When, on the day after the change of Ruler, I called on Shaikh Shakhbut in Bahrain on my way back to Abu Dhabi, he greeted me in his usual polite way and assured me that he bore no ill-will against anyone: if his family and people had decided that the time had come for him to step down, so be it. He wished his brother well in the task he had taken on. Zayid had asked him to stay away from Abu Dhabi for two years. And so he did. Zayid made generous provision for his exiled brother and welcomed him back as an honoured member of the family after two years, Shakhbut spending the remaining twenty years of his life in his ancestral home of AlAin in the Buraimi oasis. Shaikh Zayid issued an order to the family and everybody else that nobody was to tell their mother what had happened.

As Ruler, Shaikh Zayid immediately implemented the suggestions I had made for the administration of Abu Dhabi, including an Investment Board (with British, American and French members) and putting the competent and capable sons of Shaikh Mohamed bin Khalifa in charge of the brand-new government departments. Zayid carried out his first ambition, of which he had told me many times, to bring fresh water from Buraimi and to make Abu Dhabi green with grass and trees. He succeeded (much of the work being done after I left Abu Dhabi in 1968) and went on to create instant cities in Abu Dhabi and AlAin in the Buraimi oasis, improving the way of life and welfare of the people but inevitably attracting the problems of government associated with developing countries. One problem that was not solved was how to obtain the expertise and labour required for the development of Abu Dhabi without swamping the local native population with foreigners: the true Abu Dhabians now number only about 20% of the population and Shaikh Zayid has recently resorted to paying generous bonuses to local families who produce many children.

J B Kelly has described the impact of wealth more graphically in his *Arabia, The Gulf and The West*:

> *Abu Dhabi town has expanded into a kind of Arabian Torremolinos, a bloated, disordered mass of architectural vulgarities and grotesqueries, which it would take a sturdy pen and even stronger nerves merely to enumerate. AlAin... in the Buraimi oasis has had money lavished upon it out of all proportion to the size of its original population, with the result that its population has now swollen out of all recognition, as tribesmen from near and far and 'Uitlanders' of every description have swarmed in to enjoy the cornucopia.*

An Abu Dhabian's picture of Abu Dhabi before and after Shaikh Zayid's accession is contained in Mohamed alFahim's book *From Rags to Riches: A Story of Abu Dhabi* but it tends to blame the British Government for Shaikh Shakhbut's shortcomings and to become a hagiography of Shaikh Zayid. Indeed, it is difficult to be even lightly and constructively critical of the Gulf Rulers and their regimes as I rediscovered when invited to collaborate with a British academic and an Abu Dhabi research institute on a biography of Shaikh Zayid. Much work went into this, especially by the academic, who eventually and sadly told me that it appeared our effort had not found favour with the Abu Dhabi Establishment, being too objective. Shaikh Shakhbut *thought* that the British Government controlled the British Press; the Gulf Rulers *ensure* that they control the local press.

In November 1967 the Political Resident and the Political Agents in Bahrain, Qatar, Abu Dhabi and Dubai were visited by Mr Goronwy Roberts, Minister of State in the Foreign Office in the Labour Government of Harold Wilson, with an assurance from HMG that they had no intention of abandoning their Special Position in the Gulf in the near future. This statement was well-received by Shaikh Zayid, who saw it as giving him time to carry out his plans for the development of Abu Dhabi within the protection from outside interference afforded by HMG. Goronwy Roberts was back with us again in January 1968, personally appalled at the message he had to transmit: that the future could now be foreseen and HMG would withdraw from their Special Position in December 1971, when British protection would be withdrawn from the Gulf States: these would become fully independent and responsible for the conduct of their own defence and foreign affairs. Shaikh Zayid was not pleased: he told me that he felt betrayed. I hastened to reassure him that during the three years to December 1971 we could put into place the political, administrative, economic and defence structures required to support, organise and forward his development plans. The sudden volte-face by HMG was worrying: in the case of the seven Trucial States there was no cohesion, except for Abu Dhabi they were tiny in size and they had unsolved problems among themselves and with Iran and Saudi Arabia. If instability ensued, the 150 years of Pax Britannica could well be followed by Lord Curzon's prediction that "Both sea and shores would lapse into the anarchical chaos from which they have so laboriously been reclaimed."

There was, fortunately, a Council of Rulers of the seven Trucial States serviced by the Political Agent in Dubai, at that time David (later Sir David) Roberts, a true Welsh-speaking Welshman and not a mongrel like me. The two of us attended meetings of the Council and we thought that it would be within our remit to attend, as the Rulers wished, a meeting to discuss the Goronwy Roberts message. We thought that we might be helpful in explaining its import and the time scale. But higher authority forbade us to attend, a misguided order since the task of the Political Agents was to be at the side of the Rulers especially when discussing external and defence affairs; and we would be carrying out such a duty for another three years. We were "The Consul at Sunset". I left Abu Dhabi on 1 April 1968, so had little to do with later developments (except that HMG's withdrawal from its Special Position was managed by the Arabian Department of the Foreign Office and the Political Resident with the help of a "network analysis" devised by the Diplomatic Service Inspectorate, of which I was now in charge, to control the complex unravelling of the many strands of that position). Eventually, on 2 December 1971, six of the seven Trucial States joined together to form the United Arab Emirates (UAE), the seventh, Ras al Khaimah, joining two months later. But before I left Abu Dhabi it was clear that the future of the Trucial States would depend principally on Shaikh Zayid and Shaikh Rashid of Dubai, two strong personalities who dominated the Trucial Council. Although Dubai would be able to make some contribution, the financing of the Council would come from Abu Dhabi's ever-increasing oil production. Shaikh Zayid would be the paymaster, so it was inevitable that with his decisive approach to affairs he would be elected in 1971 President of the UAE with the equally direct and commonsensical Shaikh Rashid as Vice-President and Prime Minister.

The change of Ruler made little difference to the life of the Political Agent and his family. I continued to call on the Ruler to discuss matters of mutual interest but the outcomes were now mostly positive.

Shaikh Shakhbut, his family and people were of the tolerant Sunni persuasion of Islam. He granted land for Roman Catholic and Anglican Churches; the former was soon built and a priest, Father Barnabas (a superb fund raiser) installed. The Anglican Church was much slower off the mark and it was not until the time of Shaikh Zayid and the arrival of the Reverend David Elliott as resident Anglican Chaplain in Abu Dhabi for the Trucial States and Qatar that the Anglican Church was built and later consecrated by the Bishop in Jerusalem in the presence of the Political Resident, now Sir Stewart Crawford, and Shaikh Zayid. When Shaikh Zayid told his *majlis* that he would be attending the consecration ceremony several of those present enquired if this was not going a bit far for a Muslim. Shaikh Zayid told them that there was only one God, the British prayed to him too, and so would he and those around him who would accompany him to the ceremony - end of argument. I sat by Shaikh Zayid in the Church and explained the proceedings to him as well as Christening and Confirmation, causing him to express admiration for those who were received into their faith twice. He continued his examination of the Christian Church in conversation with the Bishop and David Elliott over the dinner that Christina and I gave that evening. Shaikh Zayid came alone, without retainers (the last time this happened), and early - a quite exceptional occurrence: his very late arrival had delayed the start of the consecration service that day - and when the Political Resident and the Bishop arrived they found him engaging me in a competition of rising smoothly and quickly from a squatting position on the floor. In 1966 he was an extremely nice, unspoiled man.

Christina made her own important contribution to the future of Abu Dhabi when she started, in our house, a class under Kathryn's governess for the five English-speaking children who were in Abu Dhabi in 1965. Later the British trading house of Gray Mackenzie let her have a room in their compound as the number of children increased with the influx of skilled workers to build Abu Dhabi and overflowed the limited accommodation in our house. Shaikh Zayid donated a plot of land for the Abu Dhabi Community School which thereafter went from strength to strength, despite the unhelpful attitude of the ADPC who wished to spend ADPC money only on ADPC children but had been quite happy for some of these children to be taught for nothing in Christina's pioneering class.

Shaikh Zayid also earmarked a piece of land in AlAin for a house for the Political Agent, who frequently had to visit that town to discuss matters with Shaikh Zayid. Quite different to his deposed brother and justifiably proud of his physical prowess and his skill at hunting and shooting (he beat me hollow in a clay-pigeon shooting contest) he was very much a man of the desert and would escape from the claims of government whenever he could and frequently inconveniently. His four wives all lived in Buraimi, whereas Shaikh Shakhbut had only Shaikha Mariam and she lived with him in Abu Dhabi. So his heart was in the Buraimi area, to which he escaped with or without excuse from Abu Dhaibi town. HMG never took up the offer of land or built a house in AlAin; but this probably does not matter now that there is, I understand, a dual carriageway from Abu Dhabi to AlAin and the five or six hour landrover journey of the 1960s is now reduced to an hour. I could rely on the ready and willing Army Air Corps stationed at Sharjah to helicopter me to AlAin when the urgency of the business to be done with an absent-from-Abu Dhabi Ruler made the long trek there and back out of the question. The pilot would land his machine in the Agency compound and leave his rotor turning while he had coffee or a meal with Christina and me. Then up and away and some useful instruction en route for me in the art of piloting a helicopter. Christina used to express some concern that if the pilot did not want to stop his engine when collecting me from the Political Agency, how could she be certain that he would be able to start it again when the time came for us to return from AlAin? But it always did.

When Christina and I visited AlAin for longer than a one-day visit we stayed either with the Trucial Oman Scouts in their "Beau Geste" fort at Jahili or in Shaikh Zayid's new guest house. David Shepherd made a splendid painting of Fort Jahili of which we had a copy, but it was ruined by water beyond repair during its journey from Abu Dhabi to the UK in 1968. The unusual feature of Shaikh Zayid's guest house was that the washbasins were in the *majlis* and not in the bedrooms so guests had a communal morning ablution. On one of our visits we were invited, together with other foreign visitors to AlAin, to lunch with the Ruler's brother, Shaikh Khalid bin Sultan, and were shown into a tower room in his palace. When we tried to get out, since nobody had called us for lunch and time was ticking by, we discovered that we were locked in, the retainer having turned the key in the lock as he left us. Eventually our shouting and banging brought relief but no lunch, which was gone. When I complained to Khalid about his treatment of his guests he gave no indication that he knew what I was talking about: he gave the impression of having taken perhaps too strong medication.

The Trucial Oman Scouts escorted the Political Resident and the Political Agent and their ladies when we made our tours into the Liwa Oasis, which bordered the empty Quarter of Arabia. These tours were in effect an imperial progress of some sixty people – a numerous TOS escort plus guides and servants, with Union Jacks and the Political Resident and the Political Agent flying their flags and TOS pennants on Dodge Power Wagons and Landrovers making their way, sometimes with difficulty, up and down the dunes in a beautiful desert landscape. Such a tour was supposed to provide the PR and PA with an opportunity to seek the views of the local headmen; but these were always in loud praise of the Ruler whether he was Shakhbut or Zayid; it seemed to me that we were welcomed by the local population only for the attention and medicines they could obtain from the TOS medical orderly who accompanied us. Politically the tours were pointless. Sir William and Lady Luce, and, of course, Hugh Boustead, as "old Sudan and Aden hands" enjoyed these tours and thought them important, as Lady Luce confirms in her book; but their successors, Sir Stewart and Lady Crawford, found them hard and pointless going, and Christina and I sympathised with them: good plumbing is essential for the full enjoyment of life. Our final tour in 1966 marked the end of an era; and about time, since they were no help at all in forwarding the tasks facing us in Abu Dhabi. These post-imperial processions always ended amusingly: after four or five days on tour a Scottish Aviation Pioneer of the RAF came from Sharjah to collect us from a suitable hard patch in the desert. Once again the pilot would not stop his engines on this curious ragbag of an aircraft the construction of which suggested to my ex-pilot's eye that Scottish Aviation had learnt nothing from the increasingly sophisticated machines we flew during World War Two; or even from the de Havilland Dove and Heron passenger aircraft flown by Gulf Aviation, our "local" airline. A Pioneer pilot confided to me that he kept the engines turning since no airman wished to be responsible for stranding such a distinguished political party in the desert.

The Political Agency compound in Abu Dhabi was open to all, in contrast to its counterpart in Dubai which had an armed police guard inspected every morning by the Political Agent. It was rumoured that one Political Agent, who had been somewhat left of centre in his views as a young man, was so captivated by the apparent trappings of power that he dressed the Agency servants in uniforms reminiscent of the Raj. The informality of our arrangements in Abu Dhabi proved their worth during the Arab-Israel War of 1967, when false charges of collusion with Israel were levelled against HMG. There were disturbances in Dubai and the guard on the Agency was reinforced. In Abu Dhabi Shaikh Zayid and I spent the morning in the little garden outside the Palace, drinking coffee and chatting and listening to the BBC, while a crowd of locals and Palestinians watched us in silence but took the message that all was well between us. At lunchtime we retired to our own homes and the rest of the day passed quietly without any trouble for the Ruler or the Political Agent. During this period of unrest in the Middle East Shaikh Zayid responded to the declared wish of local Palestinians to fight the Israelis by offering to pay their air fares to the front. He had quite a few takers but because of lack of airline carrying capacity they got no further than Kuwait; and most of them returned to Abu Dhabi when the war was over.

By the end of 1967 Abu Dhabi was growing fast; but Christina and I could recall that in 1965 and 1966 we included in our Christmas party all the Christian expatriates – British, American, Europeans, Northern Arabs, Lebanese and Palestinians – 85 in all in 1965 and 108 in 1966; we could not do it in 1967. So we saw the end of yet another era in the Gulf when personal relationships at all levels and with all manner of men made the world go round.

When the Foreign Office informed the Political Resident and me that I was to leave Abu Dhabi on transfer to the Diplomatic Service Inspectorate in London, Sir Stewart Crawford commented that Shaikh Zayid would not like the news and I should have to choose my moment to tell him. Fortunately my successor was James Treadwell and I drew on his surname to suggest to Shaikh Zayid that his appointment indicated "a good step" (*khutwah taiyibat* in Arabic) into the future. He expressed his regret at my departure and had it recorded in a generously worded letter, in English, which he instructed the Director of his Office to send me:

> *Abu Dhabi will miss you very badly especially at this stage when changes are seen everywhere. His Highness realises the tremendous task you have had to shoulder and appreciates the way you handled it, leaving an indelible impression on all those who come across (sic) which is really gratifying. He will certainly cherish the memories of your association with Abu Dhabi.*

Life with Shaikh Zayid as Ruler was more straightforward; but one missed the inevitably humorous and very human side of Shaikh Shakhbut's erratic behaviour, which produced many good stories, a few of which are worth retelling.

In March 1966 I reported, but not with much pleasure, to the Political Resident and the Foreign Office that Shaikh Shakhbut had taken delivery of a Rolls-Royce Phantom V Limousine. The idea of acquiring one came to him after he had inspected in August 1965 my new Humber Hawk. An enquiry to Rolls-Royce brought their reply fortunately by sea-mail. When he raised the matter with me again I suggested that he take his time since there were no roads suitable for such a prestige car and no adequate servicing facilities. Unfortunately he mentioned his interest to a visiting VIP, a member of the House of Lords and Chairman of one of the banks hoping for better things in Abu Dhabi, who rushed in to show how important and influential he was. He would arrange "through a friend of mine on the board of Rolls-Royce " for a Phantom V on show at the Motor Show in London to be reserved for Shaikh Shakhbut. Visits by British VIPs did not invariably contribute to the prosecution of British foreign policy.

Fortunately no story broke in the British press on lines of "Desert Shaikh has Rolls-Royce but No Roads" but other reports not complimentary to Shaikh Shakhbut did appear and inevitably and understandably he "blew up" and demanded the prosecution of the offending journalist and the newspaper. To some extent I could agree with part of his complaint since the tone of some articles was unnecessarily offensive. Some journalists thought that by writing such criticism they were bringing pressure on HMG to be firmer with Shaikh Shakhbut about his style of government. In fact the journalists made things worse and increased the difficulty of the task in Abu Dhabi. Shaikh Shakhbut could not believe that HMG had no responsibility for or control over the press and we became the target for some part of his resentment.

There were occasions when Shaikh Shakhbut saw and enjoyed the joke as much as I did. One day Christina and I were invited to lunch with him. We sat and sat in the *majlis* and the silences got longer and longer. Eventually the Ruler told his son, Sultan, to find out why the meal was so delayed. Another long wait until Sultan returned with the news that the sheep purchased for the meal had died and the Palace cook was afraid to tell his master, who had lost 300 rupees (£20) by this infelicitous purchase of a sheep on its last legs. This struck the Shaikh as very funny and he laughed loudly. We eventually lunched on chicken.

Once when I called on the Ruler there was an atrocious smell in the *majlis*. After I had exchanged greetings with him and, as courtesy demanded, sat in silence for a while before opening our discussions of the topics of the day, he asked me if I could detect a smell; I said I could; where is it coming from, enquired the Ruler; I replied that it was pervasive but seemed to be stronger at the end of the room where we were sitting. "Help me", said the Ruler; and together we dragged away from the wall the sofa on which we were sitting to discover a dead pigeon of some days maturity. Shaikh Shakhbut really enjoyed the laughter in the *majlis* that greeted this discovery.

I had a touching and clear indication of Shaikh Shakhbut's trust in me when I was taking him through, clause by clause and line by line, a draft tax law he had to promulgate to give effect to his 50-50 agreement with the oil companies. When we came to "invisible assets" he said that such a concept was impossible: how could one own something one could not see? The clause would have to be struck out. I persevered until Shaikh Shakhbut enquired if I understood the concept and the need to include it in the law. When I said that I did he said that since he trusted me he would agree to the law as drafted.

One day BP provided a helicopter for me to take the Ruler on an aerial tour around the island on which stood the town of Abu Dhabi. I thought that a view from the air, and from low altitude, might lead him to see where he might make improvements to his domain. He thoroughly enjoyed the flight, pointing out landmarks, and announced when we landed that Abu Dhabi was beautiful and would be spoiled by any additional building. Another ploy - and any development – frustrated. Many observers, such as J B Kelly (quoted in this Chapter), would say that the empty perfection of Abu Dhabi has been spoiled; but others would quote the truism of the omelette.

11

Diplomatic Service Inspectorate

Having spent three years trying to persuade Shaikhs Shakhbut and Zayid to take the paths of wisdom as seen by HMG, as a Diplomatic Service Inspector I should now be doing the same with the Heads of British Diplomatic and Consular Posts around the world. The Inspectorate had grown in the 19th century in response to the growth and quickening of international relations, which followed the industrial revolution. One of the first Inspections on record dates from 1850 when Lord Augustus Loftus, then Secretary of Legation in Berlin, inspected the Consular Posts along the Baltic Sea. In 1857 Consul John Green in Alexandria captured the essential qualities of Inspectors with an enviable economy of words when he recommended the appointment of Inspectors "to whom a rank should be given removing them beyond the influence of cajolery or slight, fully capable of pointing out to Consuls the necessity of alteration in their practice, thoroughly acquainted with the details of the Service in all its bearings and with instructions to do all in their power to improve the Service without personal complaints, except in extreme cases".

Consul Green was not much ahead of his time, since between 1871 and 1873 the Secretary of State, Lord Granville, asked Consular Posts to report on their establishment and duties and despatched senior members of the Consular and Commercial Departments (the latter had been established in the Foreign Office in 1866) "to make local enquiries" in Europe and the Levant. Before the end of the century similar "enquiries" had been made in the West Indies, the United States and China.

In 1905, following a Report by a Committee of Enquiry into the Constitution of the Consular Service, the Secretary of

State, now Lord Lansdowne, instructed the Heads of Diplomatic Missions to arrange for the inspection of Consular Posts under their supervision. Lord Lansdowne directed that such inspections should be carried out every four years and that the approval of the Foreign Office should be obtained in advance of a proposed inspection in order that attention might be drawn to any consulates which might require special investigation. Guidance to inspecting officers was conveyed in the form of a short (one foolscap side) memorandum which, despite its brevity, covered, in straightforward English, what "modern management science" calls Management by Objectives, Resource Allocation, Staff Inspection and Organisation and Method, but without use of these jargon phrases. The guidance also dealt with the justification for the maintenance of a Post in view of the political and commercial interest involved. But it was not until after the First World War that full-time Inspectors of the Consular Establishments were appointed with rank equivalent to Consul General.

After the Second World War the pace of international exchange again quickened and the number of independent countries with which HMG wished to maintain diplomatic relations increased. The Inspectorate reflected these changes. A Senior Inspector of Diplomatic Missions was appointed in 1944 and in 1946 his functions were combined with those of the Consular Inspectors to form the Corps of Foreign Service Inspectors. In 1963 the importance of trade promotion was marked by the addition to the Inspectorate of a Commercial Inspector. It may be noted here, for the benefit of readers who may imagine the Foreign Office and Diplomatic Service to be fuddy-duddy organisations, that in 1966 they already had a Planning Unit and a Management Services Unit (i.e. the Inspectorate), which the Fulton Committee (Cmnd.3638) recommended that year for all major Government Departments. As I have indicated above, there was already a long history of efficiency audit in the Service.

When I joined the Inspectorate in April 1968 yet another Committee of Inquiry into the Diplomatic Service was under way. This was the Committee chaired by Sir Val Duncan, the Chairman of Rio Tinto-Zinc (RTZ), whose terms of reference were, in brief, to reduce the cost of Britain's overseas representation. He proposed to do so by dividing the world into two parts: the first containing countries important to HMG (the Inner Area) and the second, those unimportant countries (the Outer Area). Such an undiplomatic and unrealistic recommendation fell flat on its face with HMG; but Val Duncan's Report contained other useful thoughts and recommendations of which the Inspectorate made full use in their continuing task of shaping the Overseas Representation of the United Kingdom to contemporary demands. Val Duncan described the Inspectorate as a valuable instrument for controlling the scale and cost of British representation overseas.

An internal change decreed by the top of the Office, immediately before I joined the Inspectorate, was the abolition of the post of Chief Inspector (the Chief Clerk had already gone and was now called Chief of Administration) on the grounds that the work of the Inspectorate could be supervised by an Assistant Under Secretary for Administration as part of his duties. Thus I found myself put in charge of the Inspectorate as a Grade 4 officer; the Chief Inspector had been in Grade 3. The task of managing the Inspectorate was soon again recognised as a distinct responsibility, which a busy Under-Secretary could not carry, and I was given the title of Senior Inspector, but no promotion.

I did not like the organisation of the Inspectorate or the over-written contents of the "Instructions to Inspectors", the "Inspectors' Bible", which had grown like Topsy over the years. I brought together the four General Inspectors, the two Commercial Inspectors and the Home Inspector, since I saw no logic in independent inspections of individual parts of the Service. All Inspectors in my view should have that "acquaintance with the details of the Service in all its bearings" to which Consul Green drew attention in 1857. I also brought into the Inspectorate an Organisation and Methods Section which had been spawned by the "management revolution" in Whitehall and the Computer Services Branch as the Automatic Data Processing (ADP) Section. By January 1970 I had under command a coordinated and coherent instrument for responding to the recommendations for the organisation of the Inspectorate made by the Duncan Committee. In this work I had the invaluable assistance of Trevor Gatty, the Senior Assistant Inspector, who was the first member of the Service fully to understand the benefits and limitations of "modern management science". I also rewrote the "Inspectors' Bible" to reflect contemporary conditions and to provide a slimmer volume. I stated the principal purpose of an Inspection of an overseas Post to be the recommendation "in the light of stated operational requirements, of such arrangements for British representation as will enable that representation to be carried out effectively and efficiently. The aim of an Inspection is economy in the true sense: the least possible expenditure in terms of manpower, money and material, consistent with policy and operational requirements, local circumstances and the good morale of the staff". I was concerned to ensure that the Inspectorate cultivated the approach to problems, which considers every part in its relation to the whole. Modern management teaching overemphasised the "either/or" approach; I wished to emphasise the "both/and" creative thinking of true management - or leadership. Above all the Inspectors should beware of too much organisation or reorganisation, "that wonderful method" as Petronius Arbiter described it in 60 AD (as quoted by Robert Townsend in his cautionary *Up the Organisation*) "for creating the illusion of progress while producing confusion, inefficiency and demoralisation".

I saw Inspection as an exercise in diplomacy, which in many ways was more difficult than dealing with foreigners. An Inspector treated with colleagues who were emotionally involved with a career which took them, their wives and families to all parts of the world (or separated them from their children in boarding school in the United Kingdom) and required them to do a wide range of jobs in a wide variety of alien climates and environments. I did not want Inspectors to lessen the creative tension, which is inseparable from all high-performing teams, but I did not want them to underestimate the strain on members of the Service; the Inspectors should try to understand the constraints and pressures, which bear upon an officer abroad. St Paul's words to the Romans ("Be not wise in your own conceits...") were particularly apt in this context. I also saw the Inspectors as having an important "communications" role. People on the periphery of an organisation can form distorted ideas of the direction and management (or leadership) of their organisation. The Inspector was an informed visitor from the centre who could do much good by spending time talking to his colleagues at

Post and their families. This was a more worthwhile employment of an Inspector's time than 'agonising reappraisals" late into the night of what recommendations he was going to make.

I was frequently surprised, when inspecting a Post, by the lack of preparation which some people made for an exercise of which they had been given generous warning, there being nothing of a surprise raid about a Diplomatic Service Inspection. At the top of the Embassy one would find an Ambassador who had no idea how he and his wife spent their income and no guidance for the Inspector on calculating the essential expenditure (frais de representation) for a Head of Mission. This Ambassador would usually have been a pre-war entrant to the Service and innumerate at that. Lower down the Embassy one would find that the Accountant did not have his accounts up to date, a state of affairs which said little for his sense of self-preservation. I also had a test for a good or bad Post. In the former case the receptionist or security guard in the entrance hall would greet me by name and say that the Head of Chancery was awaiting me; and later my secretary would report that good arrangements were available for the essential supplies of tea and coffee. In the latter case, a somewhat tired head would be raised with a query about my identity and a "I'll find out if somebody is expecting you": and the tea and coffee essentials would not be in place. Both such Posts benefited from an Inspection.

I wrote a new Order Book for the Foreign Office designed particularly to help new entrants and officers returning to the Department from overseas to understand the bureaucratic machinery. There had been an earlier Order Book but this had been swept away by the "management revolution". If a Civil Servant is to get full value from the Government machine he must know how it works; it is probably an exaggeration to say that if he gets the form right the substance will take care of itself; but there is a grain of truth, or at least of guidance, in that apparently cynical statement. With the help of Trevor Gatty and the O&M and ADP Sections we also wrote a Diary for Administration Officers to guide them day-by-day through the fifty volumes of Diplomatic Service Procedure, which their creation had spawned. We also started a rationalisation of these fifty volumes; and introduced a system whereby Posts could inspect themselves in advance of an Inspection and so put themselves on the correct lines and reduce the time and effort an Inspector would have to devote to a Post. An examination we carried out of the place of computers in the Foreign Office concluded that the Department could not afford the space, expenditure or extra staff (computers do not save staff), which the mainframe computers of the 1960s would demand. Nor did I believe that the generation which then provided the top of the Office and Ministers would accept information via a video screen: it would not be content that it had the precise information it required until it had seen the actual papers on which, say, the Foreign Secretary had recorded his views on Ruritania. Only in the Communications Department did we see a role for computers.

I spent six years in the Inspectorate, widening my knowledge of the World by visits to Russia, Poland, Roumania, Venezuela, Colombia, Ecuador, Peru, Canada, the United States, India, Japan, the Cameroons, France and Mauritius. I also gained a useful understanding of the management of an international organisation with its Head Office in London and Branch Offices in some 150 countries around the World. When I wrote my Valedictory Report in 1974, having by then been promoted to Chief Inspector and Grade 3, I offered two quotations as adequate comment on the philosophy of the Diplomatic Service Inspectorate and the qualities required by its officers. The first quotation was that from St Paul's Epistle to the Romans, which I have already quoted. The second was from Boswell's *Life of Johnson* where Boswell observes that "Sir Alexander Dick tells me that he remembers having a thousand people a year to dine at his house; that is reckoning each person as one each time that he dined there." Dr Johnson replies "That, Sir, is about three a day". "How your statement lessens the idea," says Boswell. To which the good Doctor rejoins, "That, Sir, is the good of counting. It brings everything to a certainty which before floated in the mind indefinitely."

I went on to say that I had come into the Inspectorate in 1968 at a time when a Whitehall "management revolution" spearheaded by a naïve adoption of simplistic O&M practices had thrown away many of the commonsense precepts that had grown up with the British Public Services and had put in their place mechanistic and jejune systems which failed to meet the operational requirements of the afflicted Departments. I agreed with C H Sissons, an Under Secretary in the Department of Employment and Productivity, who said in an article published in the *Spectator* on 27 February 1971, that the characteristic of recent years had been "a growth of the mythology of management". Sissons' view was that there had been a deliberate and persistent propagation of the idea that management was a new concept in the Civil Service and that analytical procedures, of a kind which had always held an important place, had now been introduced as a startling novelty to produce a new Golden Age of efficiency. "One can only compare the untiring vein of talk on these lines which emerges from influential quarters with the effusions of those, in other fields, whose pronouncements seem to suggest that sex is a novelty or that fornication has just been discovered. In both worlds, of course, there are some queer habits about and there has even been some technical change."

One point I made in my valedictory, which was particularly relevant to my generation of diplomats, was the emotional shock to a wife of her husband's appointment to the Inspectorate. An Inspector would have been in the Service for 20 to 25 years and probably married for most of that time. He and his wife would have shared all the experiences that a Diplomatic Service career could bring and would have worked together to ensure the success of his (and her) task wherever they had served. On his appointment to the Inspectorate the husband would not only have a task which would take him away from home for eight months of the year but, for the first time, a job in which the wife could play no part at all.

The Chief Clerk to whom I had addressed my valedictory report was Donald Tebbit, later Sir Donald and High Commissioner to Australia. His response was generous:

If I may say so the report contains the quintessence of the wisdom, energy, experience and good humour which has made your tenure of the Chief Inspector's seat so memorable and effective. The improvements which have been brought about through your work have been legion and I know that my predecessor was just as relieved as I have been to know not only that the Inspectorate was in good hands and heart but that we had at our disposal a Chief Inspector capable at short notice of tackling any problem and finding a workable answer to any conundrum. You will be much missed.

I recognise that six years is a long stint but I am afraid I am not prepared to bind myself or my successors never to repeat this offence. You talk of the importance of getting "round pegs for round holes"; by the same token you must concede how tempting it is to keep a round Chief Inspector in a round hole once you have got him there."

12

Ambassador to Kuwait

When Christina and I returned to Britain from Abu Dhabi in 1968 we moved back into our house in Dorking. The expression "his/her face fell" had never been real for me until I saw Christina's expression when she walked into our home. While we were away in the Gulf we had let the house through a local estate agent, who had pocketed his fees but not ensured that the tenants were treating the house and garden in the way to which these important pieces of the Lamb estate (the only pieces) had become accustomed under Christina's magic touch. Animals had been let loose, not only in the garden but in the house, and floors and furniture required much hard work to restore them to their previous immaculate condition. But this was soon achieved and we settled down contentedly to life at home, which is so superior in every way to life abroad. Christina and I could never become expatriates.

Elizabeth was now working in London; Robin was at Brasenose College, Oxford and Kathryn at a local school, moving to Parsons Mead School for Girls in Ashtead in 1970. I was away from home a lot during my early years in the Inspectorate but Christina became well integrated into the life of Dorking, taking on inter alia the responsibility of Red Cross Welfare Officer for the district. Her coat of arms at this time would have been a commode recumbent on the roof rack of a Mini.

I found the combination of my duties in the Foreign Office (on my promotion to Grade 3 I became an Assistant Under Secretary as well as receiving the title of Chief Inspector) and daily commuting increasingly tiring and broached with Christina the idea of selling the Dorking house and moving into a flat in London. Christina was all for it, since she was determined never to let her home again and it would be easier to lock up and leave a flat than it would a house and garden. We found a flat in Bayswater, selling our house to the Methodist Church for occupation as a (very modest) manse. Property prices had risen considerably between 1961 and 1973, our house going for over four times the price we paid for it and having to pay seven times that price for the London flat. We had just moved into this new home when, in February 1974, the Chief Clerk told me that I was to be appointed Ambassador to Kuwait in succession to John (later Sir John) Wilton. Before I left for Kuwait I was informed that "The Queen has been graciously pleased, on the occasion of Her Majesty's Birthday 1974, to direct that you should be appointed a Companion of the Most Distinguished Order of St Michael and St George (CMG), in recognition of the valuable services which you have rendered".

Mid-1974 was an exciting time to take over a British Embassy in the Middle East. In the autumn of 1973 the fourth war between Israel and Egypt and Syria had broken out, with support for the latter two coming from the oil-producing Arab States of Saudi Arabia and the Gulf. These States, including Kuwait, announced restrictions on oil supply to Europe, Japan and the United States. The immediate impact of this action was to raise the price of oil, make more acute the economic problems of the industrialised countries and cause severe balance-of-payments problems for those countries dependent on oil imports. Britain, more than any other country, depended at this time on Middle East oil to fuel its economy, which soon showed signs of recession, as did other economies of the Western World. John Wilton had done a superb job in persuading the Ruler of Kuwait that the ties of friendship between Britain and Kuwait should weigh heavily in the balance of the interests of an oil-exporting country and by the time I arrived in Kuwait the oil was again flowing westwards.

The oil tide had however been turning against the West during the six years I had been preoccupied with the Diplomatic Service Inspectorate. In Chapter 8 I described some of the events in the oil industry, which led to the formation of OPEC in 1960. The following decade had marked the start of the struggle between OPEC and the international oil companies for control of the production and pricing of oil. The contest had moved decisively in OPEC's favour in 1970 when the Government of Libya forced a cut in production and an increase in the price per barrel and in the Government's tax take. A year later the OPEC governments effectively secured for themselves full control over the exploitation of their oil reserves. This was followed by agreements reached in 1972 and 1973, which were designed to protect the producing countries' oil reserves from the effects of President Nixon's abandonment of the Bretton Woods parity of the United States Dollar, which was consequently devalued. By the end of 1972 the price of oil had reached $5.00 a barrel. A demand for a price of $6.00 per barrel was rejected by the international oil companies. When the Arab-Israeli War broke out in the autumn of 1973, not only did the oil-producing States of Arabia and the Gulf introduce the oil embargo, which I have already mentioned, but they also, in company this time with Iran, proclaimed the pricing of their oil independently of the international oil companies. The OPEC countries raised the price of the Arabian Light marker crude to $10.84 a barrel in December 1973. From then on OPEC was the sole determinator of the price of crude oil entering world markets.

Such was the oil situation when I arrived in Kuwait in 1974, in which year further moves on the international scene had included Saudi Arabia obtaining a 60% participation in ARAMCO, paving the way for a complete takeover of the company; the establishment of the International Energy Agency (IEA) to watch over the interests of the Western oil-consuming countries (but France did not join and Norway became only an associate member); a proposal by the IEA of a floor price of $7.00 a barrel for oil (but no mention of a ceiling price). The floor price proposal held no attraction for the OPEC governments who saw the price of their oil ever-increasing, not falling – IEA was offering the wrong guarantee – and OPEC would not consider a dialogue with the IEA. Their reluctance was not all that important since the United States, whose Secretary of State, Dr Henry Kissinger, was the driving force behind the formation and works of the IEA, refused to contemplate a dialogue with OPEC.

HMG, of course, went along with the United States Government in refusing to talk to OPEC, persuading itself that good bilateral relations with the oil-producing countries would safeguard the supply of oil on acceptable terms. A Conference on International Economic Cooperation was held in Paris in 1975 but was a total failure: it was an over-ambitious attempt to solve other world and regional economic and financial problems as well as the price and supply of oil. Meanwhile a new oil province was opening up in the North Sea, and HMG established the British National Oil Corporation (BNOC) to exploit it.

In 1976 Kuwait, along with the other OPEC Governments, took over, through nationalisation or expropriation, the remaining foreign petroleum holdings in its territory.

All this activity on the international oil front demanded patient and persistent diplomacy with the Kuwait Government; but before I could involve myself therein, I had to present my Credentials to His Highness the Amir of Kuwait, Shaikh Sabah Salim AlSabah. This I did soon after my arrival on 18 June, delivering into the hands of the Amir a Letter from The Queen, who had graciously received Christina and me before we left London:

Your Highness

Being desirous to maintain, without interruption, the relations of friendship and good understanding which happily subsist between the two Crowns, I have selected My Trusty and Well-beloved Albert Thomas Lamb, Esquire, Companion of My Most Distinguished Order of St Michael and St George, Member of My Most Excellent Order of the British Empire, upon whom has been conferred the decoration of My Distinguished Flying Cross, to proceed to the Court of Your Highness in the character of My Ambassador Extraordinary and Plenipotentiary.

Having already had ample experience of Mr Lamb's talents and zeal for My service, I doubt not that he will discharge his Mission in such a manner as to merit Your Highness's approbation and esteem, and to prove himself worthy of this new mark of My confidence.

I request that you will give entire credence to all that Mr Lamb shall have occasion to communicate to You in My name, more especially when he shall express to Your Highness My cordial wishes for Your Happiness, and shall assure You of the invariable attachment and highest esteem with which I am,

>*Your Highness's*
>*Good Friend*
>*(Signed) ELIZABETH R.*

The Amir received me kindly, mentioning his especial pleasure that I had already served in Kuwait and would know, and be known to, many of his people. Indeed, at the first reception I attended I felt a firm blow on my shoulder, to find, when I turned around, that it had been delivered by Abdulla AlGhanim, the Minister of Electricity and Water, with a "Welcome back, Archie!" (Abdulla rejoiced in his nickname of "Jock" acquired from his education as an electrical engineer in Glasgow. His Glasgow accent was impressive, as was the Geordie accent of his cousin, Abdulaziz, who had qualified as a British Master Mariner out of South Shields).

There had been little physical change in Kuwait since I left it in 1965. All the Government Departments were still in the same place and many headed by the same Ministers. I called on all of them and found no difficulty in picking up with them the threads of Anglo-Kuwaiti relations. These were becoming more complex with the welcome widening of Kuwait's international interests: her continuing pressure on the parent companies (BP and Gulf) of the Kuwait Oil Company (KOC) for increasing influence in the Company's affairs which culminated, as mentioned above, in the Kuwait Government taking over the Company in 1976; the great surge of wealth which flowed into Kuwait from the ever-rising oil prices; and the Kuwait Government's determination to step up the country's defence profile.

In this latter defence task, the Kuwait authorities had the help of the Kuwait Liaison Team (KLT), a British training and maintenance unit of twenty officers and 100 senior NCOs (there were no other ranks) of much experience and superb quality under command of a Colonel. Because of the existence of this team, for which the Kuwait Government paid (the proceeds funding the Embassy at no cost to HMG), my Embassy had no Service Attaché. This was not an entirely satisfactory arrangement for the Ambassador since the Colonel wore Kuwaiti uniform as a member of the Emirate's armed forces and could not, and would not, be put in the invidious position of refusing to advise the Ambassador on matters which touched upon his professional allegiance to Kuwait. The advice of my own service Attaché would have been welcome when we entered negotiations to sell 165 Chieftain tanks (successful) and patrol boats (unsuccessful). We did not try to sell military aircraft although the Hawk trainer-fighter was by then coming off the assembly line and would have been ideal for the State's embryo air force.

As part of our campaign to sell British military hardware to Kuwait, HMG invited the Minister of Defence and the Interior, Shaikh Saad Abdulla Salim AlSabah, the son by a black concubine of Shaikh Abdulla Salim, who ruled before Shaikh Sabah, on an official visit to Britain. I accompanied Shaikh Saad with whom I had established a happy rapport. Whenever I called on Shaikh Saad, and after we had completed whatever business we had in hand, he would open a wider subject of interest to him and spend at least as much time on this topic as we had on our immediate concern. His visit to Britain was a success, every day of the week-long visit being covered by Kuwaiti cameramen whose film was shown nightly on Kuwait State Television.

The Shaikh's visit attracted the attention of the BBC, who obtained the permission of the Foreign Office to make a programme about the work of the British Ambassador to Kuwait. In telling me by telegraph that this authority had been granted, Dr David Owen, who was then Foreign Secretary, instructed me not to justify HMG's policy. I thought this an extraordinary instruction, which betrayed some ignorance of the role of an Ambassador in presenting and explaining policy, policy which had been made by Her Majesty's Government and therefore required no justification to foreign governments, such justification as it required having been made before the Houses of Parliament. When the BBC eventually showed the film on *Panorama* it presented me as a somewhat suspect arms salesman, the only context being defence sales. This did not reflect my interview by the *Panorama* producer and reporter, which had ranged more widely over Anglo-Kuwaiti relations and trade as a whole and my part in them. The reader may be interested to know what was in my mind.

I saw my job as British Ambassador to Kuwait as being to conduct harmonious relations with Kuwait, harmonious because the two governments were not playing the same tune and could not be in unison: in musical terms the Kuwaiti tune was pentatonic in the Arab tradition whilst ours was based on the octave. The best the Ambassador could do was to produce a harmony. In order to catch the Kuwaiti tune it was necessary to grasp that Kuwait was a long-established city-state with well-rooted maritime, mercantile and financial traditions and a cohesive society. In most people's minds Kuwait was an oil-rich State (period - as our American friends say); but I also saw it as a money-generating machine driven by professional dealers who drove very hard bargains. Kuwait has always been far ahead of other oil-producing countries in moving into equity investments and was the first such state to acquire downstream oil investments abroad. The "Q8" logo on petrol stations in Britain was witness to this. Trade promotion was an important activity for my Embassy but must not exist in a compartment by itself. It arose out of the totality of our relationship with Kuwait and so my Embassy and I practised what I called "total diplomacy": we interested ourselves in everything that was going on; and I made sure that all my colleagues in the Embassy knew what that was.

In short, we nursed the constituency, and our success in trade was owed to those British companies which did the same. In three years we had quadrupled our trade (excluding arms sales) and in 1977 we were on track to double our performance of 1976. We could always do better, as I reminded our businessmen in a talk I gave in London. I told them the story of the bride on her wedding night reminding her bridegroom: "You kiss very well but should you not be doing something more?" We were paying Kuwait £600 million (US Dollars one billion) for oil and earned £143 million in visible exports in 1976. In addition there were substantial invisible earnings for Britain from the Kuwait connexion: I always emphasised the "money" side of Kuwait and was fortunate to secure the agreement of the then Governor of the Bank of England, Lord Richardson, to appoint one of his men as Economic and Financial Secretary in my Embassy. I was also conscious of the impact, on employment at home, of big hardware orders. For example, Govan Shipbuilders sold six general cargo carriers of 23,000 dwt to the Kuwait Shipping Company: I understood that this order would provide about five years work for 1500 men in the Glasgow shipyard.

The Govan contract was an interesting example of how an Ambassador and his wife can help with a major contract. I was well aware of the tough negotiating tactics of the Kuwaitis: I was not sure that the Govan Company were or that the nerve of their negotiator would hold in a triangular contest in which my South Korean colleague was also involved with instructions, he told me, "to undercut you, dear colleague, whatever price you offer". The Koreans were in a strong position since they had taken over the construction of these general cargo carriers for the Kuwaitis, and to the Govan design, a few years earlier when Govan had incredibly turned down a repeat order for eleven ships they had already sold to Kuwait on the grounds that their order book was full. Now their book was empty and they badly wanted the order for the six ships.

I asked Christina if she would be willing to put up the Govan representative in our flat above the Chancery for as long as it took to bring about a successful negotiation. I told her that I wanted to keep the guest's nerves steady and she agreed to ensure that he was properly cared for, made at home with good food, a drink when required and clean laundry on his bed when he returned from the day's haggling. His nerve did break, but only one evening after we had come home from a difficult day when it appeared to him that we would have to accept the Kuwaitis' terms. We were able to stiffen him before the next day, when we found the Kuwaitis all smiles and ready to sign on the dotted line at a price, they told me later, far above that they had hoped to screw out of Govan. My Korean colleague was intrigued rather than disappointed and questioned me for some time on the tactics I had used to defeat him. I contented myself with a little Corps Diplomatique one-upmanship about the British Ambassador deserving a little success occasionally.

Disappointing was our failure to obtain any major construction contracts during a period when Kuwait's increasing wealth had started it off again on an orgy of building and rebuilding. Most of the consultants employed by Kuwait were British, seventy British firms had resident representatives in Kuwait, and the British Community was already over four thousand strong. But our contractors were unwilling to bid for business on Kuwaiti terms. They maintained that to do so would lose them money. One assumed that the foreign contractors working in Kuwait were either suffering equally or were costing the work on a different basis, which would yield a profit. Certainly the South Korean contractors followed the latter principle, importing all their workers from South Korea, housing them in low-grade barrack accommodation and paying them what a conscript private would earn in the Korean Army.

In order to ensure that the resident British businessmen in Kuwait were kept fully briefed on what we in the Embassy knew of the local scene, my Commercial Secretary, Arthur Marshall (later our Ambassador in Aden) and I held a meeting every Monday evening in Arthur's house over a glass of beer (then still available to Embassies). Inevitably this gathering became known as "The Monday Club" (but without any of the political leanings of the London Club of the same name). After a while the businessmen lost their suspicion of one another and would exchange information short, understandably, of giving away their company's commercial secrets. This was a great success as was the open House, which Christina and I held every Wednesday evening at the Embassy for visiting and resident British businessmen and Kuwaiti and other local counterparts.

Those were hard-working years in Kuwait but the Embassy staff were superb, the skill, application and good humour of the Head of Chancery, Peter Hinchcliffe (later HM Ambassador to Jordan) being an example to us all. Humour was never forgotten in the Embassy, especially by Peter, who, in addition to writing the annual Embassy Revue, looked out for leg-pulls during the rest of the year. On 23 October 1974 I found among the morning pile of incoming telegrams the following:

> *Personal for Ambassador from Secretary of State.*
> *Many happy returns and congratulations on reaching 53 at such an early age especially in the circumstances now prevailing in the Middle East.*
> *Jim.*

Peter also contrived a spoof telegram of instructions for the Diplomatic Service Inspector, Guy Simmons, who was with us on 1 April 1976, telling him to proceed urgently to the Seychelles but without his assistant and his secretary, both of whom were to return to London. In the Seychelles he would have the assistance of a Miss Veridaniake, a Seychelloise of great beauty and warm and outgoing personality who would provide a whole range of services not normally associated with an Inspection. Guy's sense of humour was as quick as and equal to Peter's. In his spoof reply (inserted into Peter's pile of evening telegrams) he commented "I seem to remember meeting a lady of the same name (possibly her mother) during a brief bachelor visit in the early fifties". Guy also composed a calypso on the Inspectors, which illuminated several aspects of their craft.

An exceptionally successful political visit to Kuwait was that of James (now Lord) Callaghan when he was Foreign Secretary in 1975. Twenty years earlier the Ruler of Kuwait, Shaikh Sabah Salim Al Sabah, had given Mr Callaghan a set of prayer beads during the latter's previous visit to the Emirate. When Mr Callaghan called on the Amir, he produced the prayer beads, to the evident pleasure of the Amir, who said that Mr Callaghan was now entitled to a new set, giving the latter the beads he had in his hand. This simple act of memory, civility and humour got the visit off to a flying start and really did, in that frequently trite phrase, "cement the good relations existing between our two countries".

Other visitors, political and business, were not all as much at ease as was Mr Callaghan. Many of them appeared to find intercourse with the Ruler and his Ministers difficult and would compensate by becoming frightfully British and straightforward. For example, the Amir might say that he would like to do such and such and would like to do it with British cooperation. The British VIP would not say (as I, and I think any other Ambassador, certainly the French, would) that the Amir's idea was worth study and we would return to the subject as soon as possible. No, our VIP, metaphorically standing to attention with his thumbs down the seams of his trousers, would observe that he could see difficulties in the way of that idea. The Amir's eyes would cloud and that was the end of that interview. Whenever I taxed the VIP afterwards, with throwing away an opportunity, he would say that he had to give the Amir his honest opinion.

Shaikh Sabah Salim died during my time in Kuwait and was succeeded by Shaikh Jabir Ahmed Al Sabah, who had been Finance Minister and Prime Minister on his way to the Rulership. He was an impressively well-informed man, always calm, with a clear vision of the Kuwait he wished to build: a city-state not over-industrialised and using the revenues for the betterment of the future as well as the present generation. In this task of money-management he was helped by an exceptional Kuwaiti of Palestinian origin, Khalid Abu Saud, who remained at the centre of financial policy-making in Kuwait for over thirty years.

Impressive though these Kuwaitis were, the most exceptional man in Kuwait was Tariq Rajab, artist, architect, archaeologist and collector, a Renaissance man, who had the vision to establish a model British secondary school in Kuwait. Tariq had been educated at Bristol University and the Slade School of Art and was Director of the Kuwait Museum when we were in Kuwait in 1965. Tariq and his British wife, Jehan, worked hard to establish their New English School with a British Headmaster and British teachers. The standard of the school was such that our daughter, Kathryn, was able to complete her A Levels there and go on to St Hugh's, Oxford, as a Scholar. The school was popular not only with expatriates who wished their children to have a British education but also with the Kuwaitis, including an Under Secretary in the Education Department. Tariq also has his own private museum where the range of his interests and his industry as a collector were displayed to perfection.

Over the Christmas/New Year Holiday of 1977-78 Christina and I transferred from Kuwait to Norway, attending on New Year's Eve the marriage of our son, Robin, to Susan Moxon. Robin (now, in 2002, Deputy Chief of Mission in Kuwait) and Susan met while they were both in Libya, Robin on attachment to the British Embassy in Tripoli and Susan accompanying her father, an oil man. The Ambassador, Sir Donald Murray, told me that he had watched with interest and pleasure the burgeoning of the romance between Robin and Susan around the Embassy swimming pool.

13

Ambassador to Norway

At our Posts abroad, the living accommodation which Christina and I occupied had been half a flat, then a small villa in a flower garden in Rome; a small, modern and well-appointed flat in Genoa; a spacious flat in a well-built pre-war block in Bucharest (where we first enjoyed the benefits of central heating and cooking on natural gas, piped in from the Ploesti oilfields); the flat I have described at Shemlan; a jerry-built bungalow which leaked everywhere in Bahrain before we moved into a house in the Residency compound. This house was well-nigh ideal, an unusual triumph for the Ministry of Works, but spoiled by a kitchen where we had to cook by paraffin when all the Bahrainis had moved to electricity or bottled gas; the houses I have described in Kuwait and Abu Dhabi in the 1960s; and the Ambassador's "flat above the shop" in Kuwait. The Embassy in Kuwait had been completed in 1933 by the Department of Works of the Government of India to the standard design of a Political Agency, which it then was, of the Empire of India. The flat was well-nigh perfect for its purpose, roomy, homely and comfortable yet with a terrace and two reception rooms more than adequate for the entertaining required by the demands of the Post. Its terrace had once had a chandelled ceiling similar to the one I have described earlier in the Assistant Political Agent's house; but one of my predecessors had a Swedish wife who did not like the ceiling and persuaded the Ministry of Works to replace it with plastic ceiling tiles and bright white lights. As one elderly distinguished Kuwaiti remarked to me one evening, "You ruined the ceiling".

Now in Oslo we were to move into our grandest accommodation by far, a 19th Century villa built by a Norwegian banker of Swiss origins, Thomas Heftye, in the 1850s. HMG acquired the house in 1905 for £18,000 in gold, after King Edward VII had asked his daughter, Queen Maud, the wife of the new King

Haakon, which house would be suitable as an Embassy in which he could stay on his visits to Oslo (then Christiania). Another version of this story is that King Edward asked the same question of a visiting Norwegian nobleman. But the answer was the same: the Heftye Villa. I used to tell this story in my Welcome-to-the Table address (an essential part of Norwegian protocol) whenever I had an assembly of bankers, stressing particularly the £18,000 purchase price. There would follow a silence, broken by a banker's voice "And you still have a bargain!" Any reader interested in the architecture of the villa will find a comprehensive account in "*Country Life*" of 22 December 1988, written after substantial refurbishment and redecoration of the house.

Christina and I moved into this delightful house, set in its own grounds and with views so steeply down into Oslo Fjord that it seemed that the ships entering and leaving the harbour were at the bottom of the garden. We found a small suite ready for us at the top of the house but in winter we found the small study on the first floor more cosy for unoccupied evenings and weekends in winter: it had a fireplace which our private sitting room did not, a small thing perhaps but the comfort of an open fire was irresistible.

Behind the house, and hidden by it, was the Chancery building, newly built in the 1960s and housing, sensibly, all the departments of the Embassy, Ambassador's room, Chancery, Commercial Department, Economic Department, Information Department, Service Attachés (one from each Service, with a Marine Officer occasionally filling the Military Attaché's post), Consular Section, Administration Section and Registry. This was the biggest and most important Post I had commanded. Norway was an important trading partner of Britain, one-third of its exports coming to the United Kingdom, a member of NATO, with the Headquarters of Allied Forces North (AFNORTH) under a British Commander in Chief in Oslo, and one of the only two members (Turkey is the other) with the Soviet Union as an immediate neighbour, an Arctic Warfare training ground for the British Armed Forces, a member of the European Free Trade Area (EFTA) but not a member of the European Community, and now an increasingly important oil producer. It was this last element which had brought me from Kuwait to Oslo.

During my briefing in London the Foreign Office told me that Mr Callaghan, as Foreign Minister, had paid a visit to Norway from which he had returned saying, in short, "It's all right but it's not right". Because of my, by now, extensive background in the geopolitics of oil and money I had been selected for the Oslo Embassy in the hope that I would find out why "It's not right". I had never expected to be given a Western European Embassy, having been content to serve out my time in the Middle East. But the politics of oil had broken upon Anglo-Norwegian relations and it was no exaggeration to say that the only members of our Diplomatic Service with an understanding of them were the Arabists, through whose drawing-rooms (to misquote Lady Eden at the time of Suez) oil had flowed. The Foreign Office asked me to go to Oslo, assess the situation and when I had formed an opinion to return to London for consultations on future policy. Mr Callaghan, who was now Prime Minister, told me of his impressions formed during his visit to Oslo. This was a rare opportunity, almost a blank canvas on which to paint the picture of harmonious Anglo-Norwegian relations as I saw them.

After two months immersing myself in the Norwegian scene and with wise counsel from my two Counsellors, John Robson (later Ambassador to Norway), my Head of Chancery, and Colin McLean (later UK Permanent Representative in Strasbourg after a tough time as High Commissioner in Uganda), my Economic Counsellor, I came to the conclusion that impressive and important as the oil developments in the North Sea had been, they had been appreciated almost entirely on the technical level and insufficiently through political eyes. The North Sea offshore oil industry was, of course, only a few years old, the first commercial discovery in the Norwegian sector of the North Sea having been made as recently as 1969 and exports of oil starting in 1975. It was not until 1976 that significant production began in the British sector. But before I could develop my thoughts on enhancing the political aspects of the North Sea oil industry I had to examine how they would fit into Anglo-Norwegian relations and the susceptibilities of the two partners; and in order to arrive at that examination I had first to refresh my knowledge of the history of Norway and that country's relations with the United Kingdom.

My reading told me that the relationship between the United Kingdom went back a long way to a time when there was no United Kingdom but already an England, Scotland, Wales and Ireland, and no Norway but a Northland of fiercely independent kingdoms whose pent-up energies burst upon the British Isles in the late 8th Century AD. Raids began across the North Sea, carried out by men from the bays and inlets of the west coast of Norway, the Norwegian word for bay or inlet, "vik", giving us the name "Viking" for the raiders. These men were hungry for land, coming as they did from a long and narrow country with little coastal plain suitable for the plough. In 1017 AD King Canute took over the whole of England after a series of Viking raids, which began in 981 AD. The shape of England as we know it from the traditional counties began to emerge. The last successful invasion of England, by the Normans, themselves of Viking stock, in 1066 AD, owed much to the toll taken of the English army the previous week in a successful battle against the Viking King Harold Hadrada.

After these events the Vikings declined; as the historian H A L Fisher put it in his History of Europe, "The Viking aristocracy bled to death in Civil War". After the last Viking King in the 13th Century the Northmen returned to extracting a meagre living from a barren soil and the country passed under the sway of the Kings of Denmark until, after the Napoleonic Wars in the late 18th/early 19th Century, the peace treaties transferred Norway from Danish to Swedish tutelage.

The history of Norway from the 19th Century renewed the national pride of the Norwegians and reinforced their nationalism, fed as it was by the liberal regimes of the Swedish Kings, by the rediscovery of the Norse sagas and ancient legends which encouraged a break in the connexion with an alien crown. The break came in 1905 when the Storting, the Norwegian Parliament, declared that the Union with Sweden was at an end. Norway became an independent sovereign state under King Haakon

VII, who was married to Princess Maud, a daughter of King Edward VII of England, and whose son, King Olav, reigned over Norway during my Mission to his country.

Meanwhile the English had swept on through the expansion of Elizabethan England and through conquest, colonisation, trade and the impetus of the Industrial Revolution to the widest Empire and degree of world influence known to man until the emergence of the Superpowers in the second half of the 20th Century. The English, or British, acquired an understanding of the way of the world and of the interdependence of mankind, bringing an internationalist approach to their foreign policy. Trade across the North Sea developed rapidly during the 19th and 20th Centuries, especially after the advent of the steamship, which for a long time placed the British and Norwegian mercantile marines at the top of the league of sea-going nations. But this development did not make Norway any more internationalist in outlook. Its foreign policy, until after the First World War, was to have no foreign policy in order to avoid foreign entanglements. Norwegian ships largely operated away from Norway since the country generated relatively little cargo and the fame, strength and prosperity of the Norwegian merchant marine was based on cross-trading. Nor did maritime fame bring prosperity to the Norwegians: in the 1920s Norway was the poorest country in Europe.

In modern times - and it is the immediate past which has perhaps the most recognisable impact upon present attitudes, though I would not discount the influence of older historical developments - Anglo-Norwegian relations had been based on trade, seafaring and fishing, together with staunch brotherhood in times of trouble and crisis. The United Kingdom and Norway became bound in a relationship of mutual affection, respect and understanding. One could say that there was an Anglo-Norwegian love affair; but then into this Anglo-Norwegian Garden of Eden had slithered the serpent oil, the most politically divisive commodity in international trade.

The first approaches by the British and Norwegian Governments to the prospect of oil wealth under the North Sea started well with the successful negotiation of a Median Line down the North Sea delineating the British and Norwegian Sectors. (This negotiation was virtually complete when I left the Foreign Office "oil desk" in 1965; in 1978 I had the honour of signing, together with the Norwegian Foreign Minister, Knut Frydenlund, the final protocol for the last 300 metres by latitude 62 degrees North). The two Governments continued well with the unitisation of the Frigg, Statfjord and Murchison oil and gas fields which straddle the Median Line and which have been jointly developed to the two countries' mutual benefit and to the profit of the two governments and the national and international oil companies involved. It was not until the two countries reached the stage of the provision of goods and services for the North Sea offshore industry that the serpent made his appearance.

The two governments had done well in adding, to the firm foundation on which relations rested, the extensions built of politico-legal bricks, which formed the Median Line and the Unitised Fields. The extension made of mercantile bricks had not got off the ground. One reason was a serious psychological barrier formed of the words "offshore" and "Continental Shelf". When these words first became important in the British and Norwegian commercial vocabulary, they appeared to suggest to British and Norwegian businessmen that they must discard their traditional trading connexions and seek government support and access to, and government protection in, a new and mysterious market, which, although only just off their shores, was out of reach. Indeed, the British Government had even introduced into their export trade statistics a new destination, "The Continental Shelf", a prime example of bureaucratic ignorance of the real world: nobody on any Continental Shelf buys anything; mainland traders buy and sell the goods and operations. The two Departments of Energy had established a Joint Working Party designed to study the provision of goods and services but its deliberations had become a dialogue of the deaf. The British Department of Energy seemed to believe that British exporters had a prescriptive right to supply the Norwegian offshore industry; the Norwegians, whose petroleum policy was nationalist in the extreme, regarded the offshore industry as a forcing ground where Norwegian industry could grow and eventually supply not only its own oil and gas industry, but could compete in similar markets around the world. Britain had long accustomed itself to living in an international contest and to accepting that foreign companies might establish themselves in Britain to contribute to the British economy where they might anchor knowledge, technology, skills and employment even if they exported their profits.

The Norwegian Government would have none of this; and the spirit of 1905 was important: the date was still very near to the hearts and minds of the Norwegians and they were jealous of their independence and of their nationalism. This had created for them the dilemma of a country torn between national and international energy interests, with the former predominating. Arrogant in its ignorance of the international oil world, Norway drew back from full membership of the International Energy Agency (IEA) and, alone of the Western Allies, it rushed into a relationship with the Organisation of Arab Petroleum Exporting Countries (OAPEC). Norway had also saddled itself with a State Oil Company, STATOIL, which became a state within a State, a political instrument, providing an increasing amount of the State income and leading Norway, with the not indifferent acquiescence of the Norwegian Trades Union Organisation (LO) and the Labour Government towards a Corporate State, in which Statoil would supply money, the LO control the work force and the Government make laws and rules which would suit principally these three main players. Norway was the outstanding example of a country where nationalism and the desire to extract maximum advantage for the State and the State Oil Company had placed Norwegian oil policy at one remove at least from commercial reality. (These chickens came home to roost in 1987 when a scandal erupted around Statoil's gross mismanagement of the financing of a new [always unnecessary, in my view] refinery at Mongstad on Norway's west coast.)

My briefing in the Foreign Office had also told me that the Norwegian Government had run up an international debt of US $26 billion for its four million people; $6500 per person to be compared with Britain's international debt of around $350 per person at that time. When oil production began for Norway, that normally level-headed country decided that the millennium had arrived and that every Norwegian's standard of living and income could be increased; but the oil industry did not produce the disposable profits on the scale anticipated or as quickly as forecast. Combined with a sacrosanct Scandinavian Welfare State philosophy and agricultural and industrial subsidies to virtually everyone who asked for one, such profligacy led, inevitably, to a rise in inflation, which soon overtook Britain's and made Norway the high-cost country of Europe with daunting financial and fiscal problems facing its Labour Government.

Having absorbed all this information, I came to the conclusion that the reason why "it was not right" was because the two Governments lacked a continuing political overview of the offshore oil industry and where it was leading the two countries bilaterally, multilaterally and internationally. One would not obtain, as the British Department of Energy seemed to want, a change of Norwegian policies to accommodate British ambitions; but one would have a better idea of what historical and modern impulses were moving the Norwegians, while bringing the latter to value the benefits that could accrue from close cooperation with their ally across the North Sea. I saw no reason for the two governments to become embroiled in quarrels about goods and services when much greater and deeper issues affecting not only the two countries but also the whole Western Alliance was at stake. This was the time when NATO took the decision to station in Europe intermediate range nuclear weapons in response to the Soviet Union's massive deployment of similar weapons, and when the industrialised West was still reeling from the increasing oil prices, to be raised yet further in 1979. So convinced was I that the course of the meetings between the two Departments of Energy would lead to a quarrel that I tried to stop a junior British Energy Minister from coming to Oslo. I failed, he excelled in irritation and I have never seen a member of a foreign government so angry as was the Norwegian Minister of Petroleum, after a lecture by an over-confident British representative. A Norwegian Under Secretary and I decided to desert the official luncheon offered by the Norwegian Ministry: we took the two Ministers off to a quiet lunch where we succeeded in patching up relations between them.

I decided that I would first try my ideas for a political overview of the offshore oil industry on the Foreign Minister,

Knut Frydenlund, a wise and patient man who sadly died in 1982 at the height of his powers. He listened to my proposals, we discussed them, he welcomed them and added: "This is the first time a foreign Ambassador has outlined my policy for me". I could not resist replying: "But it is the British Ambassador", and we parted, as always, on the best of terms.

I then returned to London, explained my proposals to the Western European Department and went over them with the Foreign Secretary, Dr David Owen. After he had accepted them and appeared to value my efforts, he spoiled the impression he had given by remarking: "I suppose I have to give you what you want; you seem to be rather popular in No 10." Although disappointed by this unnecessary spikiness on the part of Dr Owen, I was naturally pleased to hear of Prime Minister Callaghan's confidence in me.

I returned, well pleased, to Oslo and briefed my two Counsellors on the way ahead for the Embassy, which brought from Colin: "Well! I've never heard of an Ambassador writing his own brief and persuading his own and a foreign government to accept it!"

I was glad that I had agreed with HMG the role and purpose of my Embassy, since the oil world soon burst again into one of its periodic crises.

In April 1978 the Afghan Communist Party carried out a coup in Kabul, but failed to establish itself as a firm government of the country. The Soviet Union sent a military team in 1979 to help stabilise the regime and followed this with a full-scale military invasion of Afghanistan on Christmas Day 1979. A war between Soviet and Afghan Government forces and Afghan freedom fighters/rebels was under way. In September 1978, President Carter initiated the Camp David discussions, which led in 1979 to a peace treaty between Egypt and Israel and to the estrangement of Egypt from the Arab World, which thereby lost its natural leader. During 1978 popular disaffection in Iran with the Government of Shah Reza Shah Pahlevi produced a wave of strikes, which by the third quarter of the year were affecting Iranian oil production. From a level of nearly 6 million barrels a day production fell to 235,000 barrels a day by the end of the year. This level of production was insufficient to meet domestic demand let alone export contracts: the shortfall was made up from increased Saudi production, which reached 10 million barrels a day in December 1978. In January 1979 the Shah abdicated, his regime toppled and the security system, which the United States Administration had tried to establish in the Gulf, based on the supposed "island of stability", provided by the Shah's regime, crumbled. On 1 February 1979 the Ayatollah Ruhollah Khomaini returned to Tehran from Paris and established a radical regime based on direct clerical rule.

The high level of Saudi production, in December 1978, was not maintained into 1979 because of a limit of 8.5 million barrels a day, placed by the Saudi Arabian Government on ARAMCO's production. Until Iranian production recovered, the international oil market began to notice the absence from the market of some 5 million barrels a day of Iranian export crude; the price levels agreed at an OPEC meeting in December 1978 (the meeting looked for a 10 per cent increase during 1979 in the price of the Arabian Light marker crude from $12.70 to $14.54) were soon left behind by the "spot" market, which by mid-February 1979 was pricing Gulf crudes at $21 a barrel and $23 a barrel by the end of that month. In March OPEC agreed to bring forward to the second quarter the marker price of $14.54 they had agreed for the last quarter of 1979 and further agreed that its members could impose such additional surcharges they deemed "justifiable in the light of their own circumstances." Saudi Arabia added no surcharges except on some high quality crude but all the other OPEC producers did.

Saudi Arabia had exceptionally permitted production for a time at 9.5 million barrels a day in the first quarter of 1979 to help make up the shortfall from Iran. This extra 1 million barrels a day was withdrawn from April 1979, partly because of increased Iranian production and partly, it was thought, to show displeasure over the Camp David Agreement between Egypt and Israel, Saudi Arabia having already broken off relations with Egypt. At around this time the effects of the cessation of oil exports from Iran began to make themselves felt in the market place where the consumers found themselves queuing for gasoline. The evident shortage of oil resulted in a further jump in the "spot" price to $33 a barrel in May.

The United States Administration had not been slow to react politically to the Soviet invasion of Afghanistan on 25 December 1979. On 23 January 1979 President Carter declared, in his State of the Union Address, the Carter Doctrine warning against any attempt from outside the region to take over the oilfields of Arabia and the Gulf. In June 1979 the United States Administration announced the formation of a Rapid Deployment Force (RDF) designed to back the political message of the Carter Doctrine with military power earmarked for the defence of the friends and interests of the United States in Arabia. The United States decision to establish this force was also influenced by the need to alleviate the shock suffered by the traditional rulers of Arabia from the United States' failure to support the Shah of Iran, America's chosen instrument for security in the Gulf.

To try to alleviate the market pressures for higher prices the Saudi Government let it be known, before an OPEC meeting in June 1979, that they were considering raising their output again. The Saudi Government were concerned at the inflationary and recessionary influences the oil price increases were having in the Western industrialised countries. The OPEC meeting finally agreed a marker price of $18 a barrel with permission for members to impose surcharges up to $5.50 a barrel. After the meeting Saudi Arabia raised its production to 9.5 million barrels a day. In September 1979 the Nigerian Government broke through the $23.50 "ceiling" and set off a further round of price increases. In December the price of Saudi marker crude, Arabian Light, was raised from $18 to $24; in January 1980 to $26; and in April 1980 to $28, at which price it stayed although OPEC agreed, in June, a theoretical marker price of $32 a barrel with surcharges permitted up to $5 a barrel, establishing a new "ceiling" of $37 a barrel.

These high prices, a miscalculation by the OPEC Governments compounded by a certain amount of panic in 1979 among the Governments of the Western industrialised countries who feared for their oil supplies (but there was plenty of oil available), did not last long. By mid-1980, over-production by the OPEC producers, unprecedented high stocks of oil in the industrialised countries and the effects of a recession in those countries resulted in a fall in the demand for OPEC crude from 28.5 million barrels a day to 27 million a day and a fall in the "spot" prices of African crudes of some $5 a barrel below official levels. In September 1980 OPEC initiated discussions aimed at designing a "long-term" strategy for the production of oil and for the pricing and escalation of oil prices according to agreed formulas. This was a significant meeting since it recognised the price of Saudi Light Arabian crude oil for the first time as the official marker price (at $30 a barrel). The wider aims of this meeting were, however, set at nought by the outbreak, in September 1980, of the war between Iran and Iraq. Exports of these two countries' oil through the Gulf soon ceased and some 4 million barrels a day of crude oil was removed from the international market. The actual effect in volume terms of this interruption in supply was small: before the war started there was a surplus of 2 to 2.5 million barrels a day in the market and the Arabian producers had to raise their production by only one million barrels a day to meet market demand. Most of this million came from Saudi Arabia, whose production was now running at 10.3 million barrels a day. But at the next OPEC meeting, in December 1980, the Arabian Light price was raised to $32 a barrel and a theoretical marker price set at $35 with permitted surcharges of $5 a barrel resulting in an OPEC "ceiling" price of $41 a barrel.

    During December 1980 Iran and Iraq began exporting crude oil again. Despite indications that
- a) the non-Communist World's demand for oil was falling from some 50 million barrels a day in 1979 to 48 million in 1980 and 46 million in 1981;
- b) non-Opec production was increasing steadily from 20 million barrels a day in 1979; and
- c) squeezed by (a) and (b), OPEC production was falling (from 31 million barrels a day in 1979 to 23 milion in 1981),

- OPEC continued its policy of maintaining high prices for oil. This policy benefited the higher cost non-OPEC oil producers such as Britain and Norway but forced consumers to look more carefully at the cost-effective use of oil and how much they could afford to buy, especially after the World moved into recession.

The Soviet Union and the United States, the Superpowers, had little or no effect on the evolution of events, except in a negative or aggravating sense. Iran and Iraq were able to start a war close to the Soviet Union's sensitive southern frontier and to the West's major store of energy (Arabian oil); the Soviet Union had nothing to show for two years of war in Afghanistan; and any security policy which the United States might have for the region was in shreds. Regional and World affairs were shaped not by the Superpowers but by countries whose principal and perhaps only export to the World was oil.

Such were the geopolitics of the international oil situation during my three years as Ambassador to Norway and the essential background to the adventure in oil in which Britain and Norway were separately and together engaged.

In addition to trade and oil, defence loomed large in the relationship. Although it was manifest that the Norwegians were ready "to leap into the snow and kill Russians" as one of them put it, they were not at all keen on NATO's wider strategy, especially where it touched on nuclear weapons. The Norwegian Government had declared Norway a nuclear-free zone and refused to allow NATO nuclear missiles to be stationed on its soil. The shock of what had happened to them during and after the German invasion of 1940 was still evident but it had made them more nationalist in relation to their defence, as with all their policies. Except where they could obtain promises of help in an emergency without having to accept the stationing of foreign troops in Norway. Thus the British Marine Commandos, together with Dutch Marines, the Royal Navy and the Royal Air Force exercised annually in Norway; and occasionally a United States Marine battalion would join an exercise. In one such exercise a United States Marine detachment, mostly black, not very happy in Arctic conditions, allowed the attacking force (British and Dutch) to pass through their lines on the evidence of the advancing troops speaking English! The umpires sent the attackers back 600 metres, a penalty which I thought most unfair. On another exercise, when, after a most civilised night aboard HMS Ark Royal, I flew in at dawn with the attacking helicopter-borne force, I spent the morning with the British troops, crossing the lines at lunch time to spend the afternoon with the Norwegian defenders. The Norwegian Colonel complained to me that the British were advancing too fast! There was no doubt that our soldiers, sailors and airmen were impressive and seemed to me to have a cutting edge much sharper and more carefully honed than that of the Norwegians. Our young Marines who formed the Commandos, and who learned to ski with full military kit on their backs in only three weeks, gave the impression, even when they were standing still, that they were slightly off the ground, leaning forward and ready to go. The Marines were not above testing out the Ambassador on snow-shoes and in a snow hole; I think I passed their tests.

I was able, one memorable evening, to mark the defence connexion between Norway and the United Kingdom when His Majesty The King accepted an invitation to dine at the Embassy in the company of the Commanding Officers of the British units which regularly exercised in Norway. My Service Attachés were also present at a unique occasion marked by the friendly informality of King Olav, who attended unaccompanied by any retinue. His Majesty's reception of me earlier, when I presented my credentials to him, was also relaxed and friendly, although we were both in dress uniform, naval in the King's case. (My uniform had been specially altered to fit my girth and grade for this occasion, the only time I wore it in Norway). The King greeted me with a smile and "I see you have a DFC" in a tone suggesting what better qualification could I have to be the British Ambassador at the court of a King who, when Crown Prince, had been the Commander-in-Chief of His country's armed forces during the Second World War.

On another occasion when we visited the Frigg field together we were both wearing flat caps. Whenever I saw him off at the airport on his annual visit to London he would be wearing a bowler hat; I do not know what headgear he wore to the Saturday afternoon First Division football match which was always a feature of this visit to London.

The King was always to be seen on Remembrance Sunday on the balcony of the Home Office, watching the Service at the Cenotaph in company with the Queen Mother and other members of the British Royal Family. His informality could cause problems: King Olav was 75 in 1978; before I left for Oslo early that year HMG asked me to discover if there were to be any celebrations of this anniversary involving our Royal Family. When I made enquiries of the King's Private Secretary, he told me that His Majesty would have corresponded directly with The Queen and in his own hand on such a matter. Indeed, all became clear and HRH the Prince of Wales came to Oslo for the celebration of the Royal Birthday. The King also had the charming habit of drinking a toast, "skoling", with every Ambassador individually during the annual banquet he gave for the Diplomatic Corps. Since this meant The King rising more than forty times to raise his glass to his lips it was an immense act of courtesy. A man to inspire affection and trust, adored and admired by the Norwegians, who were ever ready to remind one of the King's youthful prowess as a ski jumper and of his continuing skill as a yachtsman at which he had won an Olympic medal. King Olav may well have been the only true Tory left in Europe: believing in the maintenance of sensible privilege for those who enjoy it and compassion for those who do not.

The Embassy in Oslo was the setting for the most unsuccessful dinner party Christina and I ever gave. The Bishop of Fulham and Gibraltar (as his See was then called) was to pay a pastoral visit and he was to dine at the Embassy. Christina and I invited the Head of the Norwegian Lutheran Church and his wife, the Roman Catholic Bishop Gram, Archdeacon and Mrs Horlock of St Edmund's Church in Oslo and the Norwegian Minister of Church and Education (yes; and in that order). We looked forward to an evening of good cheer blessed with Christian brotherhood. The Anglican and Roman Bishops, who had known one another for years, arrived together dressed almost identically in their black and red. Bishop Gram told me that as a young priest he had spent some time at a seminary in Wales and as part of his fund-raising activities he had sold chickens in Swansea market. We were therefore able to establish a joint point of reference. Eventually we were all seated at table, I made a suitable "Welcome to the table" speech and the first signs of disaster appeared. Everything was going wrong in the kitchen for our cook, Jane, who never, before or after that evening, was forsaken by the patron saint of cooks. The food was not of the standard that even the most fundamentalist Christian could have enjoyed. The Christian spirit finally deserted us when the Minister rose, as senior Norwegian guest, to make the traditional "Thank you for the food speech". He did not mention the food but launched into a political dissertation, which could not be regarded as ecumenical or friendly against the Church, its bishops and all its workings. Christina and I were more than relieved when he took his departure, after which we apologised to our clerical guests for the food and for the Minister's lapse from grace. The Bishops were generous in their forgiveness; but Christina and I still remember that evening with a shudder.

The Minister's behaviour did, however, point to an unfortunate feature of the Norwegian: he (or she) believes that he is always right and must give you his unvarnished views. On another occasion Christina was discussing with a typical young career woman, who had no compunction in depositing her child in a crèche during the working day, the changed attitudes in wives and mothers. "Your generation has had it," quoth the young Norwegian. "You are finished." I was reprimanded one Saturday evening by an irate lady guest who had just dined at our table to celebrate a weekend visit to Oslo by Sir Walter Marshall (later Lord Marshall of Goring) and Lady Marshall, the Norwegian authorities having asked me to arrange the occasion. "You should never invite us on a Saturday; it is not done here" she almost spat at me, her embarrassed husband, the Secretary of the Norwegian Science Foundation, who were the Marshall's official hosts, standing mute behind her. I never saw either of them again nor did the Secretary send me an apology. A Norwegian joke against themselves illustrates this self-absorbed trait of this earnest people. A Texan farming delegation visited Norway and its members were distributed around Norwegian farms. At one farm the Norwegian invited the Texan to ride around the farm. In fifteen minutes the tour was completed and they were back at the farmhouse. "Why!" said the Texan, "That was remarkable. Back where I come from it takes me all day to ride around my farm." "Ja! Ja!" answered the Norwegian, "I too once had a motor car like that!" Or, if asked to write an essay on Love, or The Elephant, or any universal subject, the Norwegian will inevitably write on "Norway and the Norwegians".

As the saying goes, you can always tell a Norwegian; but you cannot tell him much.

There were many British visitors to Norway during the three years Christina and I were there, but none more welcome than HRH The Princess Anne (The Princess Royal), who came in her capacity as President of the Save the Children Fund on the occasion of the annual appeal by radio and television for charitable contributions. One item on the programme, which combined the Princess's interests in industry and charitable works, was to the Aker Engineering Group where the Directors showed a film aimed at generating interest abroad in Norway and all its works. The film was self-indulgent in the Norwegian style and brought from Princess Anne the very Norwegian-style comment "That was not a very good film, was it?" to which the Aker Directors had to agree. A delightful lady and a considerate house guest, the Princess looked particularly attractive one evening when she was going to dine (alone) with her Royal Norwegian cousins. I asked if it was permitted for an Ambassador to tell a Princess how lovely she looked; Her Royal Highness dropped me a curtsy and said "Thank you, Sir!". At that time Princess Anne was being given an unjustified rough ride by the British press, which some of the Norwegian papers were not slow in copying, seizing upon "little Eivind", who, supposedly a sick child, popped up everywhere during the Princess's tour of a children's hospital, as an example of an eager child ignored by the Princess. The truth was that he had received the Princess's attention in a room out of bounds to the Press, radio and television.

Princess Anne's visit was the only Royal Visit which Christina and I had the honour to arrange. We went a long way in preparing for the visits to Arabia and Iran and to Norway by The Queen but were transferred from Kuwait and Oslo respectively before the visits took place.

In inter-government relations the most important and effective visits were those by Lord Carrington as Foreign Secretary and Sir Michael Palliser, who was then the Permanent Under Secretary of the Foreign Office. These visits were important for two principal reasons. The first was that in response to the massive deployment of Soviet intermediate-range missiles, NATO had adopted the so-called "dual track" approach, which called for prior negotiations to ban the weapons altogether and to make their deployment dependent on a failure of the negotiations. I have already mentioned the Norwegian Government's attitude towards nuclear weapons; it was essential that they should fully understand and support the "dual track" approach and put out of their minds a proposal, which had been floated and supported by the Soviet Union, for the formal declaration of a Nordic nuclear-free zone. This was also the time when HMG decided to acquire the Trident submarine-based nuclear weapons system, a decision on which my United States colleague, the late Louis Lerner, and I made, on instructions from our Governments, a joint demarche to the Norwegian Prime Minister, who confessed to being much impressed by such solidarity (a word which was, incidentally, a shibboleth of the Norwegian Labour Party and Trades Union Congress).

The second reason was that, as I have recounted earlier in this chapter, I had persuaded the British and Norwegian Governments of the importance of a political overview and had consequently adjusted the functions and diplomatic course of my Embassy. I wished to see if my Mission would stand scrutiny by the very top of the Foreign Office. We came out of it well, comments coming back to us from our visitors reassuring us that Norway was of prime importance to the United Kingdom and that the Embassy was clearly working effectively and happily with a clear sense of purpose.

1979 was quite a year for me since, in the Birthday Honours in June, I was made a Knight Commander of the Order of the British Empire (KBE) and later in the year I was promoted to Grade 2 of the Diplomatic Service. Ambassadors who reach Grade 2 are automatically made Knight Commanders of the Order of St Michael and St George (KCMG) but it is most unusual for a KBE to be awarded to an officer in Grade 3, as I was in June. Teddy Youde (later Sir Edward and Governor of Hong Kong, sadly dying during his tour of duty there) was then the Chief Clerk and told me that the KBE was the Diplomatic Service's "battle honour". The Central Chancery of the Orders of Knighthood asked me to return my MBE badge now that I had been promoted in the Order. I explained that it had been stolen on its way from Dorking to Kuwait in 1965. In that case, said the Central Chancery, you must reimburse the Chancery with the cost of purchasing a replacement badge: £24.66, please.

Teddy Youde also had a kind word to say about my promotion to Grade 2: "this is in large measure a tribute to the splendid work which you have put into building up Anglo-Norwegian relations to a new level of importance."

My Information Officer, Peter Chandley, celebrated my KBE with the following verses (with apologies to Stanley Holloway):

ALBERT

We've a fine Head of Post, christened Albert
But nobody uses that name.
'E were wonce but a clerk oop in t'Archives,
But now 'e 'as risen ter fame.

As such, he were sent out to Norway
Ter galvanise Embassy Staff;
'E's given 'em all an 'igh profile
And soomtimes permits us to laugh.

'E's well known to Knut and to Torbjorn
To get their support in UN
And if they don't give it, and sharpish
'E'll be down there tomorrow again.

And when he cooms back to his office
You can't see the walls for the maps
Of Arctic and Barents and Svalbard –
He's been there, wearing flat cap.

When 'e were there he went flying;
He's already won t'DFC.
But he didn't impress his young daughter
"He sure scared the hell out of me".

> *When t'Navy came sailing up t'fjord*
> *He challenged them, on t'tennis court.*
> *He wasn't surprised at the outcome:*
> *Embassy-six; Navy-nought.*
>
> *There's won other Albert in Oslo*
> *Who's Mayor of that beautiful town.*
> *In Winter they both get together*
> *To cut London's Christmas tree down.*
>
> *When t'Queen heard about this achievement*
> *She said "What a wonderful tree;*
> *Send My Albert, the cutter, to see me,*
> *I'll see that he's Lamb, KBE."*
>
> *And when they came oop to t'Palace*
> *Our Queen, she got out Her sword*
> *But just as she made for to Knight him*
> *Our Albert cried "Queen, please, a word."*
>
> *It's true I were christened plain Albert*
> *But nobody uses that name.*
> *My friends - all the world - calls me ARCHIE.*
> *Said t'Queen, "Then I'll do the same".*

(The references to Knut and Torbjorn are to Knut Frydenlund, the Foreign Minister, and to Torbjorn Christensen, the Political Director of the Foreign Ministry, "down there" in Peter's verse).

As I mentioned earlier, plenty of humour is essential for a happy Embassy (Squadron or Ship), and there was plenty of it in Oslo. Andrew Palmer, who succeeded John Robson as Political Counsellor and Head of Chancery, was the principal scriptwriter; but occasionally we went outside the Embassy for inspiration. For example, we put on, three nights running in the Embassy ballroom, for the entertainment of the Embassy family, the Diplomatic Corps and British and Norwegian friends in Oslo, a performance of "The Hollow Crown". We had four readers: Christina and me, Mervyn Jones (another Welshman), who was my Chancery Secretary, and Peter Chandley. Singers included friends from the British Council and St Edmund's Church Choir, the Church organist, John Carroll, providing the piano accompaniment. Jane Chandley, Julia Jones, Christine Chesshire, my Secretary, and Ole Andersen, the Embassy butler, worked hard behind the scenes. The *Saga Weekly Post*, an English language newspaper, said that the audiences were "particularly impressed with the great versatility and professionalism displayed in this amateur theatrical." This was actually the second time Christina and I had put on "The Hollow Crown." The first time was in Kuwait when the Lord Mayor of London, Sir Murray Fox, visited us. With our friends from the British Community who were interested in theatre, we decided to put on something special for him. (But what he appreciated more than anything, when he arrived in the Embassy from three days in Saudi Arabia, was a cup of tea and a piece of Christina's home-made Dundee cake. Poor Sir Murray could not abide Arab coffee and suffered a facial spasm whenever he politely raised a cup towards his mouth without drinking).

The Embassy ballroom was not only a boon for amateur theatricals and musical recitals - when The King came to dinner we arranged an entertainment by a British lady flautist and a Norwegian harpsichordist who had made his own instrument - but also for seminars and conferences on commercial and financial matters designed to develop Norwegian relations with British industry and the City of London. I insisted that at these business occasions, formal presentations should be restricted to the morning; lunch would then be served and in the afternoon the participants could stay for as long as they liked in informal discussion. A whole day of lectures is too much for busy men.

Once a year the ballroom lent itself to a parade of beautiful models participating in a fashion show in aid of the Red Cross. Two hundred and fifty ladies attended this show; and not many less came to the annual general meeting of the Anglo-Norse Society, which was always held during the Christmas season so that the Society could sing carols and enjoy Christina's home-made mince pies after the serious business was over.

The ballroom was also the scene for one exceptionally important event in Anglo-Norwegian relations: the signing by the

British and Norwegian Ministers of Energy of the treaties regulating the unitised oilfields of Statfjord and Murchison which straddle the Median Line in the North Sea.

Once a year the Embassy Ballroom came into its own when the Commander in Chief AFNORTH (General Sir Peter Whiteley followed by General Sir Anthony Farrar-Hockley) let me have for one evening the dance band section of the military band, which was paying a visit to AFNORTH. One year the band was from the Gloucestershire Regiment and another from the Green Howards, of which King Olav was colonel. This was a useful representational occasion, to which members of the Norwegian Cabinet and Opposition were happy to accept an invitation, apart from the pleasure it gave to us and to our guests: Norwegians love to dance and, unlike myself and I suspect most British men, Norwegian men know the correct steps to every dance, waltz, foxtrot, tango, rumba, whatever you want, and execute them perfectly. Christina was able to fit in 120 guests for a dinner and dance, arranging the tables in the large and small dining rooms and in the drawing room. A contribution to the Regiments' Band Funds seemed a small price to pay for the uplift which live music of the highest standard brings to such an occasion.

At last the time came for me to retire from the Diplomatic Service. Andrew and Davina Palmer gave a farewell dinner party for Christina and me at which he recited "An Undiscovered Fragment from Tennyson's Nordic Period":

The good Sir Archie's Table, man by man,
Is gathered here, with lovely wives in tow.
For saddest motive since his scheme began,
Tomorrow homeward both the Lambs must go.

Sad, and yet we can each one of us rejoice
Who's worked within this Knight's dynamic realm.
So it's for the whole Round Table that I voice
Thanks for Sir Archie's efforts at the helm.

For us down there at Thomas Heftye's Place
It's been a privilege, and not mere toil,

> *To follow Archie at the cracking pace*
> *He sets on NATO, politics and oil.*
>
> *And at the Storting and the MFA*
> *At NUPI, and among the nation's press*
> *Norwegian friends well know his special way*
> *Of carrying out official business.*
>
> *And if by chance you haven't thought it through*
> *Or if to detail no account is paid*
> *Of matters grave – then all the worse for you –*
> *His disagreement won't be left unsaid.*
>
> *Now if it's arms control you badly want*
> *All right: but this remember well,*
> *The Lamb interpretation of détente*
> *Is that without defence it leads to Hell.*
>
> *With his fair lady, he has thrown himself*
> *At subjects all – the simple and the hard.*
> *He understands the Continental Shelf*
> *And piloted the Palmers o'er Svalbard.*
>
> *Once, "slowly answered Arthur from the barge*
> *The old order changeth, giving place to new".*
> *Your faithful Knights, in posts both small and large,*
> *Sir Archie and Christina, will remember you.*

The political message in Andrew's verses was not, I am sure, lost upon Mrs Gro Harlem Brundtland, now Norway's Prime Minister and then Leader of the Labour Party, who was among the guests together with her husband, Arne, a staunch supporter of the Conservative Party, father of her four children, and a distinguished member of the Norwegian Foreign Affairs institute (NUPI in the fourth of Andrew's verses).

A particularly touching farewell gift came to me from Group Captain A R Mason on behalf of the Air Force Element at AFNORTH: a small vase commemorating the 60th Anniversary of the founding of the RAF with a note to say "A very small token of appreciation to our departing "airman" of whom we are justifiably proud."

Erratum: p.170, first para. after verse, line 2, should read "...Mrs Gro Harlem Brundtland, later Norway's Prime Minister..."

And so home to Dorset where in 1978 we had bought a house in preparation for our retirement. Elizabeth was now working in the Prime Minister's political office in 10 Downing Street, Robin was a Second Secretary in the Embassy in Jedda and Kathryn was in her last year at St Hugh's. Christina and I were not yet grandparents. Those pleasures (now twelve of them) were still to come.

14

Envoi for an Envoy

A letter dated 2 February 1981 from Sir Michael Palliser, Permanent Secretary at the Foreign and Commonwealth Office and Head of the Diplomatic Service:

Dear Archie,

I was very glad to have the opportunity of saying goodbye to you personally when you returned here from Oslo. But I should now like to write to you formally to thank you for the many years of good work and loyal service which you have given under the Crown.

You have had a long and outstandingly successful career since joining the Foreign Office in 1938. It would not be an overstatement to say that your rise from Clerical Officer to Ambassador has been an inspiration to many, showing what can be achieved in the Service by someone with your gifts and qualities. These, together with your extensive knowledge of the international oil industry and of export promotion work, ensured the notable success of your Missions to Kuwait and Oslo during a period of momentous change in the world economic scene.

Throughout your career, Christina has supported you with energy, cheerfulness and charm. We are very grateful to her too. I know your many friends in the Service would want to join me in wishing you both a long and happy retirement.

Yours ever,

Michael.